# SCOBIE

DEDICATED

To

P.J. and P.R.

Scobie carves his way into a sucking pig at a Melbourne party given in his honour on the eve of his departure for England. On his left is jockey Bill Williamson.

# SCOBIE

## LORIN KNIGHT

NEW HORIZON

ISBN 0 7125 0101 0

Published and printed by
NEW HORIZON (Transeuros Limited)
BOGNOR REGIS
GREAT BRITAIN

# ACKNOWLEDGEMENTS

I wish to thank the many people who helped me in the preparation of this book.

Sir Gordon Richards generously found time to relate interesting anecdotes concerning some of his charges during his career as a trainer.

Some of the jockeys who rode alongside Scobie in earlier days proved to be a valuable source of stories. Jimmy Lindley and Joe Mercer together recorded their reminiscences; thereby providing an amusing insight into Scobie's personality and portraying him not only as a respected rival, but also as a friend. Jockey and trainer Colin Williams gave me valuable information about the days when both he and Scobie were closely associated with the great sprinter Be Friendly. Epsom trainer Geoff Lewis and his wife kindly invited me to meet them at their splendid "Thirty Acre Barn" training stables and answered my many questions with much good humour.

My thanks also to the many members of the press who helped and encouraged me, including Tony Stafford and Howard Wright of The Daily Telegraph; Jack Millan of The Daily Mail; Claude Duval of The Sun; and the many helpful people at The Daily Express, most especially Hilda Marshall who readily shared her enviable expertise as a racing statistician and gave me much assistance.

I must also express my thanks to The Racing Information Bureau, to Louise Gold; Tony Fairbairn; Ron Baker; and to Julia Cowe for occasionally sharing her office with me. My especial gratitude to Peter Squibb who spared no effort in bringing this book to publication. I am indebted to him for all his help and kindness.

And finally many thanks to my secretary Betty Nicholls for typing my handwritten manuscript.

The author wishes to thank the following for their permission to reproduce the photographs in this book:

Daily Express
W.W. Rouch & Co. Ltd.
The Press Association Ltd.
Central Press Photos Ltd.
Keystone Press Agency Ltd.
S & G Press Agency Ltd.
The Associated Press Ltd.
Associated Newspapers
Daily Mirror Library
Elisabeth Dudgeon

# CONTENTS

# INTRODUCTION

The history of British Racing presents us with a long list of the names of famous men who, in their time, captured the interest and imagination of the Racing public. Some of these men were illustrious, and a few notorious. Even fewer were taken to the hearts of the people in admiration and affection.

One of the few to achieve this distinction was Arthur Edward Breasley, the Australian jockey who came to ride in England in 1950. From that time, up until the late nineteen-sixties, the Racing page of any newspaper would almost invariably include the name - A. Breasley. But to his friends, and soon to the racing world at large, he was, and would always remain "Scobie".

At the time when Scobie arrived in England, the country was striving to achieve a social and economic stability lost to it as a result of the Second World War. Yet in spite of many difficulties, the early nineteen-fifties were all set to become a glamorous, and somewhat frivolous era, for England was still en fete for her freedom. This boredom with austerity extended to all aspects of the British way of life and its effects were to be felt as much on the Racing scene as elsewhere.

At Royal Ascot, fashions reflected the mood of the day. The Summer meeting at Goodwood took on the air of a garden party and even a small Park meeting called for the wearing of a hat, gloves and other smart accessories for the ladies. Nor did the gentlemen escape the dictates of fashion and custom, and it would have been a brave man who ventured into the Members' Enclosure, or even into the parade ring if he were not wearing a hat.

This was the age of the house party, the night club, and cafe society in its hey-day. "Hutch" played and sang sentimental songs at Quaglino's and all the world danced into the small hours, on dance floors of postage stamp dimensions. The champagne flowed in this world of silk and chiffon and for those rich enough to participate, this was truly a time of wine and roses. For the less fortunate members of society, life was less congenial. Wages were abysmally low, yet in spite of the hardship existing in many quarters, the spirit of the British people was riding high. With the War over and rationing at an end, life seemed to hold the promise of brighter, more prosperous days ahead. It was all rather reminiscent of the end of the reign of Queen Victoria, when her subjects, who had been Victorians, suddenly became Edwardians, and gaiety was the order of the day.

This was the England to which Arthur Edward Breasley brought his wife, May, and young daughter, Loretta. And on the day they arrived in this country, no one could have predicted the impact that this man, already several times champion jockey in Australia, would have on the British Racing scene.

Scobie had come here to ride as first jockey to Noel Cannon at the powerful Druids Lodge stable situated on Salisbury Plain, and housing the large string of horses owned by the flour magnate - Mr. J.V. Rank. The race-going public viewed this appointment with interest and were eager to see what this newcomer to the British Turf would accomplish in the coming Flat Racing season. Not that the appointment was greeted with unanimous approval, however, for there were those who would have liked to see an English jockey take the retainer at Druids Lodge, and weight was added to this argument by the fact that, as rumour had it at the time, the Australian jockey did not wish to remain in England for more than a year or so. That he is still with us some thirty years later, must surely be one of the greatest pieces of good fortune ever to befall the British turf. But in the

Spring-time of 1950, no one knew, perhaps not even Scobie himself, that we were about to witness a true genius in action.

If we take Racing statistics alone, we find that a number of jockeys rode more winners than Scobie. But statistics do not tell the whole story and it must be remembered that he did not appear on the British Racing scene until he was thirty-six years of age, with an established career as a jockey in Australia already behind him.

The English are justifiably proud that their nation has produced some outstanding jockeys. A few whose brilliance has immortalized them in the archives of British Racing and when the question arises as to who was the greatest jockey of all time, it is around three Englishmen that the controversy mainly revolves. The great Fred Archer, Gordon Richards, knighted in 1953 for his services in Racing, and Lester Piggott, who like Archer, had his first ride in public at the age of twelve. However, when the matter is raised in Racing circles, almost invariably a fourth name is brought into the discussion. That name is Arthur Edward "Scobie" Breasley.

Just how did Scobie win such vehement support from those who claim that he was the greatest jockey of all time? A claim made not only by admiring supporters, but also by knowledgable Racing men; though certainly never by Scobie himself, who is the most modest of men.

It is not difficult for anyone who watched him ride his way to fame through the nineteen-fifties and sixties, to understand why he won such public acclaim; for Scobie was much more than an accomplished jockey, he was that even rarer phenomenon, a truly fine horseman. His rapport with the horses was ever apparent and no horse was ever treated by him as an inanimate racing machine, but always as a living creature which he had teamed up with in an attempt to do the best they could on the day. His judicial use of the whip was much admired and reflected his own attitude to race riding. Scobie enjoyed winning races through the employment of his considerable skills. To have flogged a horse past the winning post would, in his eyes, have been almost as unthinkable as doping the animal. A master of the art of riding with hands and heels, he used his whip only when he considered it necessary to remind his mount of the business in hand. Scobie had perfected the art of race riding, the horses responded to him and so did the Racing public.

It is interesting to note the diversity of personality between the men who have gone down in history as the great jockeys of the past hundred years. The legendary figure of Fred Archer comes across as an unhappy man who, for all his greatness, ended his life in tragedy. While in more recent times we find the genial, much loved Sir Gordon Richards, of whom Scobie, first jockey to Sir Gordon's stable for many years, said "He is one of the best and nicest men I have ever met". Many share in that sentiment, for this small, charming man, as opposite in temperament and physique to Archer as anyone could be, won a permanent place in the affections of the Racing public. And if Lester Piggott, at first glance, gives the impression of being somewhat dour and reserved, he, nonetheless, has a very special place in the hearts of his supporters, many of whom have followed his fortunes since the days when he was the "Boy Wonder" of British Racing.

Scobie is different again from any of these other great men of the Turf, yet one suspects that there is something of each of them in his character, although he is probably a more complex individual than any of them. It was not too easy for the British race-goer to weigh up the man from "Wagga Wagga" during his early days amongst them. Used to watching their jockeys grow up from

4

apprentices, Scobie appeared to them as something of an enigma. Tall for a Flat Race jockey, he possessed the type of physique which was so well proportioned that unless he stood near to a tall person, he did not appear to be lacking in inches himself. Not an easy man to describe, and an even more difficult one to photograph. For some inexplicable reason the lens of a camera seemed to be incapable of capturing a true likeness of Scobie. He was certainly not handsome in the conventional sense of the word, yet his appearance was pleasing, with a certain charm that caught the attention. This may have owed much to the fact that while for much of the time he had a rather serious expression, he would suddenly smile, such a disarming smile, that any suggestion of severity was dispelled in an instant.

One might well suppose that one jockey mounted on a horse would look much the same as any other, especially when they are dressed in more or less identical clothing. However, as any regular race-goer knows, nothing could be further from the truth, and Scobie mounted on a horse seemed to possess a certain extra dimension, an elusive quality for which there is no name. He looked exactly what he was, a supreme genius in the saddle. The record books show that he won more than two thousand races in Britain. What they do not tell us is that he achieved this in his own beautiful and inimitable style.

Scobie's expertise as a jockey was much admired and many of his supporters wanted to know of the man himself. As a figure in the public eye, each detail of his life became of interest to someone, a fact that Scobie did not always find agreeable, being essentially a very private person. Yet those who came to know him were not disappointed. They found him to be a quiet man, never a seeker after the lime-light, and always happy to return home to his wife and daughter at the end of a busy day. In marrying a girl who had no connection with racing before her marriage, Scobie surely backed a winner, for May Breasley created a happy and secure home in which her husband, who for much of his time inhabitated a world where the pressures were often very great, could relax, set aside his public image and simply be himself.

Scobie emerges as a man of many parts. Like a many facetted diamond, there is still a touch of mystery about him. He came here as a stranger, and won, not only many races, but also a firm place in the hearts of the British Racing public, who were quick to detect the sharp intellect, ready wit and warm heart that lay beneath his quiet facade. It would be foolish to claim that he was without his critics, yet in the balance they were overwhelmed by his admirers. Sometimes he was cursed, more often he was praised. And at the end of the 1980 Flat Racing season, when he announced his intention to retire from training, many were saddened by this decision, for it seemed that a man who over the years had established himself as an almost indispensable part of the British Racing scene, was about to disappear from what might well be described as his natural habitat. Happily he remained very much a part of that scene when he embarked on yet a third career. This time as racing manager to Mr. Ravi Tikkoo.

In many ways Scobie is like an adopted son who has grown so very dear to his new family that most of the time they forget that he was not born to them. As a jockey, and subsequently as a trainer, he served British Racing well and today he is a much loved and respected figure, both on and off the Turf. This is his story....

# AN AUSTRALIAN BOYHOOD

Arthur Edward Breasley was born on 7th May 1914 in the town of Wagga Wagga which lies about midway between Melbourne and Sydney in the Australian province of New South Wales.

The name of this town referred to the aboriginal's imitation of the cry of a crow on the wing and is generally accepted as meaning "many crows". This is also reflected in the armorial bearings of Wagga Wagga which consists of a green shield with the head of a Merino ram at the base, supported on either side by gold collared crows. It bears the motto "Forward in Faith".

The original settlers soon established a strongly sheep dominated area and as far back as 1891 there were no less than 2,427,319 sheep in an area of 2,650,000 acres, though this was drastically reduced by the drought of 1902.

The sporting links of Wagga Wagga go back to the days of her early settlers and the Murrumbidgee Turf Club was established in 1960, being named after the river on whose banks the town is situated.

"We have succeeded in making ourselves famous" said the Wagga Wagga Advertiser after the Ten Mile Race was run in 1868. But perhaps this was notoriety rather than fame, and the editor himself admitted to some disquiet about the length of the race.

All the horses who had taken part returned spur marked, some to a frightful extent and one horse was so badly affected that he had to be propped up to save him from sudden death.

There was no doubt that this race was run in deadly earnest for the recorded time of the winner was twenty-three minutes, thirty-five seconds! The Murrumbidgee Turf Club never staged such a long race again.

Although still mainly an agricultural area with sheep, cattle and wheat, Wagga had progressed a long way from its humble beginnings by the time that little Arthur Breasley was born. The town now boasted a population of around 6,500, with 1,500 occupied dwellings. This was largely due to the passing of the Closer Settlement Promotion Act. Under this Act, three or more settlers could enter into negotiations for the purchase of land on which they wished to settle. On the Crown valuation of the farm ninety-five per cent was advanced by the Government Savings Bank and thereafter annual instalments of five per cent were payable, until the whole indebtedness was discharged in thirty-eight years. As a result considerable acquisition of property took place in the Wagga district.

Wheat production had by this time reached a comparable importance with sheep and the cattle population was also increasing.

Away from the agricultural scene several secondary industries had grown up. Added to this, the southern district of Wagga could boast many fine residences with delightful gardens and the railway link to Tumbarumba, built in 1915, functioned as a tentacle into that region and brought many products to Wagga, thus making it into a main marketing centre.

But for the Breasley family, it was horses and cattle that figured largest in their lives at the time when their second son was born, for Scobie's father had begun his working life as a cattle drover but through a deep interest in horses, had gravitated towards the training of trotting ponies and soon found plenty of scope for his talents in his horse loving home-land.

The new addition to the family was greeted by his two fond parents, three sisters and a brother, and although he did not know it at the time, horses were not far away from him on the day of his birth, just as they would never be too far from him for the rest of his life.

In this horse orientated world, elder brother, Bonnie, was already a young rider with dash and style. He would have liked to have had a brother who could be taken out and put on the back of a pony there and then. But the tiny scrap which Bonnie saw lying in its cot did not look like very promising material to the young boy and it seemed that he would have to wait an eternity before he could show off his skills to his little brother.

However, the time flew by, and little Arthur was hardly out of napkins before he was being initiated into the art of handling a pony. His father took him onto the driving seat of a sulky pulled by a trotting pony, and his big brother, who had already set his heart on becoming a professional jockey, was always ready to display his own considerable skills in the saddle, which the younger boy was quick to imitate.

Even without these strong influences in his early life, it is still probable that his skilful horsemanship would have predominated, for Arthur Breasley was a natural horseman equally accomplished when riding bareback as when using a saddle.

Physically, nature might well have designed him just for the purpose of becoming a jockey, for his small stature was coupled to a deceptive strength which, along with an independent spirit, made up the necessary requirements for a professional rider. However, this independent streak could sometimes land him in trouble and did so quite literally on one occasion in his extreme youth. His father, bringing home a new and untried horse, found his youngest son waiting in the stable yard. Tying the horse up before going into the house, he warned the boy that on no account must he try to mount this animal. It might have been more prudent to say nothing, for this admonition proved to be nothing but the spur which served to push the boy towards a forbidden delight, and no sooner was his father out of sight than young Arthur jumped up on to the back of the new horse. He may have intended to remain sitting there until his father's return, but the horse had other ideas and promptly threw Master Breasley on to a nearby manure heap.

But it would have taken a far greater set-back to turn this boy away from his delight in horses and riding. He was raised in a horse conscious country; his brother became an apprentice jockey while he himself was still a young child and it was almost inevitable that he would develop an interest in the Racing world. As a schoolboy he soon found his heroes among the jockeys and trainers of the day. A leading trainer at that time was Jim Scobie, and many people who observed the boy's preoccupation and skill with horses, predicted that he would become "another Scobie". The nickname stuck, and he has been "Scobie" ever since.

Long before he was old enough to leave school he was getting some experience of real racehorses by riding out on the gallops with the string of horses from the local Wagga stables of S.H. Biggins, for by this time brother Bonnie was first jockey to that trainer.

Scobie's heart and soul were in racing and being with horses. It was for this reason that school and Scobie did not go well together, for he wanted to spend every possible moment with his beloved horses and lessons seemed like an intrusion upon his time. This must have been very trying for his teachers, as he had a bright lively mind and a quick grasp of any subject that he could be per-suaded to apply himself to. But for the young Scobie, school was a place from which he wished to escape at the earliest possible moment and this he did by leaving at the age of twelve, although he was not really legally entitled to do so until two years later. Whatever regrets those responsible for his education may have had at that time, it is certain that the boy himself had none, for he felt free to get on with the real business of living and that for him meant a life with horses.

The trainer who was to launch Scobie on his winning way was the man who knew what it takes to be a champion. Pat Quinlan himself had, in his earlier days, been a professional cyclist; he had also managed the great professional runner, the famous "Blue Streak" - Jack Donaldson, one time world record holder for one hundred yards. It was one of the Quinlan horses - Noogee - that sent an excited fourteen year-old Scobie into the winner's enclosure for the first time. This took place in August 1928 at the Weribee Track in Victoria. It was to be the first of many winners but although there were signs of an embryo greatness even in those early days, Scobie still had a lot to learn. When reading newspaper reports of his early races, the British race-goer of today might be forgiven for thinking that they were all invented. Surely these tales of rough riding, crossing other horses and other mis-demeanours could not refer to the A. Breasley known in Britain for his smooth sophisticated methods. Yet it was all true. Happily for Racing, Scobie was quick to learn and built the craft into the much admired style of his later years, and long before leaving Australia he had become one of the best riders that country had ever seen.

From the beginning he learned to pace his mounts to a furlong-by-furlong time schedule and the sharp bends and short straights of his native tracks soon taught him the advantage of sticking close to the rails - a technique he was often to employ on British racecourses.

Scobie never doubted that he would become a jockey. From early childhood this had been his ambition and when this was realised it was to bring much satisfaction, not only to the young jockey himself, but also to his many admirers.

Those early days as a jockey in the country of

11

his birth were a happy time for Scobie, his large close family were proud of his achievements, though Scobie always maintained that brother Bonnie was the greater rider of the two Breasley boys. Unfortunately, Bonnie was forced out of the Racing game due to weight problems, something which his younger brother was, happily, never to experience in the whole of his long riding career.

Scobie loved sport in almost every form; he particularly enjoyed tennis, both as a player and as a spectator. He joined a tennis club and played whenever he could find the time. He was often to look back on his decision to join that club as one of the most fortunate he ever made, for it was at the tennis club that his attention was caught by the vivacious, fair-haired teenager who also played a good game of tennis. Scobie lost no time in making the acquaintance of Miss Florence (May) Fisher and so began a courtship that was to result in a marriage that has been a success story for more than forty-five years.

When the young couple met, Scobie was already well established in his career as a jockey, but May Fisher knew nothing of racing and was uninterested in horses, but this made no difference to her feelings for Scobie and many years later she paid him a charming compliment when saying that marrying him had been the best choice she had made in her life. Scobie and May were married on the 5th November 1935.

The nineteen-forties saw Scobie as a popular and successful rider in Australia, and he was to visit the winner's enclosure more than a thousand times before leaving his native land. He took the coveted Caulfield Cup no less than four times and the Sydney Cup twice, though he never did win the most prized of all Australia's Racing events - The Melbourne Cup.

A popular figure with the Racing public, he performed another type of jockey-ship when as a disc jockey he ran his own radio show. Although he had become one of his country's best riders he was, nonetheless, rated rather less than a world-beater and by his mid-thirties many felt that he was coming to the end of his career. The Australian Racing public loved to see a dare-devil in action and although Scobie replaced any early recklessness with highly developed skill and cunning, there were those who felt that because he no longer took the same risks he had taken "in his prime" he was not such a good jockey as he had been. It is their misfortune that they did not realise just how good he really was and they did not keep him long enough to find out. By the time Scobie was thirty-six years of age several Australian riders were already successful in England and the millionaire miller - James V. Rank - had heard that Breasley was a very useful sort of rider. Impressed with the riding of Scobie's fellow countrymen, who were riding on British Turf, Mr. Rank cabled an offer that was to bring Scobie to England for the first time at the start of the 1950 Flat Racing Season and thus another boyhood ambition was realised.

Mr. Rank had originally concentrated on jumpers, but was becoming increasingly interested in the Flat. It is doubtful if he could have made a better choice than that of Noel Cannon to be his trainer or of Scobie for stable jockey. Before accepting this very attractive offer, Scobie talked the matter over with his wife and family. Scobie and May had a school-age daughter Loretta to consider, and were faced with the decision of whether or not her education should be interrupted at that point. In the end it was felt that her studies could be taken up quite happily in England and in fact a visit to a new country would be nothing but beneficial.

No doubt there was some reluctance to put so much distance between himself and other members of his family, but Scobie had, by that time, been a professional jockey in his homeland for almost a quarter of a century and he, along with most Australian riders, had always seen England as the mecca of horseracing. The opportunity to ride in this country was just too good to be missed and a most suitable and rewarding way to bring to an end his very successful career. So the decision was made. One year of riding in England, to be followed by his retirement from the saddle. It all seemed to be a most suitable ending, but happily for Racing it was not to be.

If Scobie had dreamed of coming to Britain, his first impressions of this country may have been more in the nature of a nightmare, for having recently left his native Australia with its warm, sunny climate, the shock of the English Winter was considerable when he disembarked accompanied by his wife and young daughter, to be met by the grey skies of a country where the hours of sunshine were counted, and where there were very often none to count. Perhaps it was just as well that the little family arriving that day could not have been aware that the Summer of 1950 would prove to be one of the wettest on record, with a rainfall for the months of July to September being the heaviest since 1869.

Added to this, the economic and political state of the country were as gloomy as the weather. Strikes abounded that year, starting with a strike of 1,800 dockers in the Port of London on the 19th April, called as a result of three men being ex-pelled by the Transport and General Workers Union for their part in the strike of July 1949. Troops were sent in, and reinforced as the majority of the dockers came out. This strike, the third in twelve months, was denounced by the Minister as "clearly Communist inspired". The strikers were told that unless they returned to work, their services would be terminated. After this the strike collapsed.

But on 24th June a strike began at Smithfield Meat Market which lasted until 11th July. Troops were again used to keep essential services in opera-tion. Then on 13th September a strike began against the recruitment of women conductors and the Transport and General Workers Union's refusal to submit to the London Transport Executive's one pound a week claim. Again the Minister blamed Communist agitators recently expelled from their unions. And if all this were not enough, before the transport strike was concluded, the gas supplies in the North Thames area, the very area in which the Breasley family had taken a flat, were seriously diminished by yet another strike. This time it was the gas maintenance men who were refusing to accept a wage increase negotiated by the Confederation to which their unions were affiliated. Scobie may have felt some sympathy for these strikers, for he too had for some time followed the somewhat unlikely occupation for a professional jockey of a gas maintenance mechanic. This was due to the Australian government's decision during the Second World War that all able bodied citizens of that country who had not been taken into the armed forces, should be employed in work which was essential to the nation. So Scobie became a gas maintenance mechanic, and to quote him - "A very good one too!"

If the state of the country during Scobie's first year in Britain sometimes made him feel like catching the next plane back to Australia, he would, had he acted on that impulse, have been well advised to steer clear of his home town of Wagga Wagga. For 1950 brought flooding to that city, said to be comparable to the great flood of 1925. The people of Wagga had considered that any serious flood danger was gone with the completion of the Burrinjuck Dam. But in 1950 in the main street of the city, water had risen to twenty-seven feet during one afternoon and entered 1,300 buildings, while eight feet of water swept through other parts of the city, causing 1,800 people to be evacuated from their homes. No longer could the river Murrumbidgee be seen, just one vast sheet of water as far as the eye could see across North Wagga, flowing at a terrific speed.

1950 also saw the start of a most disturbing international incident when communist troops crossed into territory of the Republic of Korea.

This was the start of the Korean War, and both Britain and Australia, along with the rest of the world, were deeply disquieted by the magnitude of this affront to world peace.

With so much unrest to contend with, it is hardly surprising that many of the British public turned to sporting events in order to obtain some light relief. Yet here too they suffered several disappointments. In the Test Matches the West Indian cricketers won three tests out of four. While in motor racing, the British cars failed to beat the crack Italian models, and British heavy-weight boxing champion, Bruce Woodcock, was beaten by the American, Lee Savold, in June. The Open Golf Championship was won by A.D. Locke, of South Africa, who had also won the title the previous year.

Scobie, who has always found tennis to be the greatest spectator sport, faced the disappointment that year of seeing fellow countryman F. Sedgman beaten in the final of the men's singles championship at Wimbledon by B. Patty of the U.S.A.

But for Britain a glimmer of light flickered through the gloom, for her athletes had a most successful year in running, jumping and cycling and a women's hockey team came through the international tournament at Johannesburg in July without a single defeat.

As for Scobie himself, he may have believed in the old adage "Start as you mean to go on" for he won on both of his first two mounts in England. First on Promotion in The Ocean Plate, and then on Decorum, in The Molyneux Cup. Both these successes were scored at Liverpool, which in those days still staged Flat race meetings as well as those under National Hunt Rules.

But 1950 was not the happiest year for British Racing. The race course executives were worried by a sharp drop in attendances, as much as fifteen per cent in one year. Nor had the English horses

17

won back the predominance shown by the French during the late nineteen-forties. This was to be yet another year of triumph for horses from France, who won every classic race bar The Two Thousand Guineas, won by Palestine, a grey Fair Trial colt, who had a brilliant record as a two-year-old, having won six of his seven races in 1949. However, at the age of three, this colt could just stay a mile and not an inch more. His short head victory in the first classic of the season was largely due to a brilliant piece of opportunist riding on the part of his jockey Charlie Smirke, who never lacking in self esteem, and always at his best on the big occasion, kept Palestine in a handy position throughout the race, had him perfectly balanced at the Bushes, and drove him down into the Dip as hard as he could go, using the downhill impetus to gain a lead of almost three lengths on Prince Simon, who did not handle the descent as smoothly, but fairly flew on meeting the rising ground and was fast closing the gap on the weakening Palestine. Smirke brought the grey colt home to victory by a very short head. This had been such a masterly piece of riding that Charlie, his ego much inflated by this success, was, according to trainer Marcus Marsh, quite insufferable for days afterwards.

Smirke was only one of the many "characters" that Scobie found himself riding against during those early days in England, and a list of his contemporaries must surely strike a nostalgic note in the memory of many a race-goer of that time.

Gordon Richards, who was destined to become a great friend and respected colleague, still had several years to go before he would retire from the saddle and take out a trainer's licence. Undoubtedly, Scobie intended to challenge his supremacy on the British Turf; a challenge which Gordon accepted in good part, while still showing every intention of defeating it. Having topped a double century for the ninth time in his career by riding two hundred and forty-four winners by the end of the 1949 Flat Racing season, he had every reason for optimism.

Lester Piggott, born on the 5th November 1935, the day that Scobie married, was at the age of fifteen years, already a force to be reckoned with and no doubt felt capable of showing the newcomer from Australia a thing or two. As a result, the early encounters with Scobie were somewhat fraught. This came as something of a shock to Lester, who had grown accustomed to a certain amount of indulgence from the senior jockeys. And while no one would deny that his riding was boisterous, sometimes to the point of being downright dangerous, he had often escaped retribution on account of his extreme youth. Scobie, however, held the view that anyone old enough to compete, must also be old enough to observe the rules of the game. The clashes between the two jockeys amounted almost to a vendetta and the stewards of The Jockey Club found it necessary to intervene and caution them both.

Many years later, seeing them together as trainer and jockey and observing the understanding and respect that has developed between them, one has to smile at the memory of those early days.

Another young jockey at the time was Manny Mercer, tipped by many to become a future champion. That this ambition would sadly never be realised, though he was runner up once, may have been largely due to this young man's untimely death at the age of twenty-eight, when the filly Priddy Fair slipped and fell on the way to the start of The Red Deer Stakes at Ascot in September 1959. Mercer not only hit the rails as he fell, but being entangled in the reins, was kicked twice in the head by the frightened filly. He was killed instantly, bringing to an end a career which had unfolded like a fairy tale. For Manny had been born into a large family in the northern city of Bradford. His was a poor family with no horseracing connections at all. His father was a coach painter, and when Manny left school at the age of fourteen, it was to go into one of the local mills as a bobbin boy, which meant that as bobbins were cast off by the machines, the bobbin boys had to crawl underneath and recover them. Boys of short stature were considered most suitable for this menial task and if Manny cursed his lack of inches at that time, it was not to be very long before he would bless the day that he was born a small child who would grow into a man of well below average height. When the boy decided to visit a local fair, he could not have foreseen the far reaching results this action would have, yet this simple entertainment was to be the means by which Manny Mercer would find a new direction to his life.

A big attraction at this fair was a mule, said to be unrideable, and any boy who could stay on its back for a given number of minutes would receive the princely sum of five shillings. As a small charge was made for each invariably unsuccessful attempt, the owner of this cantankerous animal thought himself to be on money to nothing.

After several boys had been swiftly thrown to the ground, a tiny boy came forward to take his turn. He mounted the mule and to the astonishment of the onlookers remained on its back for even longer than the given amount of time while the animal employed every trick it had ever learned in the art of discarding riders. But it had met its match.

Not long after, Manny Mercer began his apprenticeship in a racing stable. He displayed a wonderful natural ability as a rider and has left his indelible mark on the Racing scene. He married Susan, daughter of trainer Harry Wragg. Their daughter Carolyn, is now married to champion jockey Pat Eddery. And although Manny never fulfilled the prophecy that he would one day be champion jockey, one cannot help thinking how very happy he would have been to know that his brother, Joe, who became a jockey largely through Manny's influence and encouragement, became champion himself for the first time twenty years after losing his elder brother on the tragic day at Ascot.

Scobie admired Manny Mercer, for he soon found the young jockey to be a fair, if exacting rival. And among the many floral tributes at the funeral which took place in Newmarket, was a wreath bearing the message "To a perfect little gentleman. A truly gentle man". This was Scobie's last tribute to Manny.

Two other famous jockey brothers who were well established in British Racing when Scobie came to ride in this country, were Eph and Doug Smith. In their case also, one would go on to be champion jockey and the other would meet with a tragic end to his ife, though the circumstances were very different from those of the Mercer brothers.

Doug Smith was a very popular character. He never won The Derby or The Oaks, and Epsom was far from being his favourite course. Yet during his career as a jockey he rode 3,111 winners - a figure surpassed only by Sir Gordon Richards whose total was 4,870. Doug won the jockey's championship five times - twice he beat Scobie for the title, once in 1958 and 1959.

Elder brother Eph bore a strong physical resemblance to Doug. He rode his first winner in 1930 and unlike his younger brother, he rode a Derby winner. In fact this colt, Blue Peter, was perhaps the best horse he ever rode, though others claim that this 1939 Derby winner was not to be compared with the highly-strung Aureole, on whom he won the King George and Queen Elizabeth Stakes. He excelled in long distance races and won The Gold Cup twice. Unlike his genial brother, he sometimes seemed lonely and depressed and deafness did not help to make life easier for him. On

12th August 1972 Eph Smith was found dead in a shallow brook near Newmarket. He was fifty-seven years old. At the inquest a verdict of misadventure was recorded.

If Lester Piggott did not have a brother to share his experiences as a jockey, he did at least have a cousin riding during Scobie's early days here. This was the able and charming Bill Rickaby, who, if he did not rank along with the truly great jockeys, was nevertheless a good sound rider. A man of true integrity, deservedly popular both on and off the race course, he was blessed with the Rickaby good looks, as was brother Fred who left England to become a trainer in South Africa. But Bill remained in his homeland and was called up for military service during the Second World War, and while many jockeys lacked the appropriate physique for service in the armed forces, Rickaby attained the rank of Major in the Royal Artillery. Sadly this intelligent, likable man was involved in a disastrous car crash in Hong Kong, which not only nearly cost him his life, but has left its mark on him ever since.

Another jockey riding in Scobie's early days here, and destined like him to become an Epsom trainer, was Birmingham born Ken Gethin. Never among the names at the top of the jockey's table, yet a very capable rider and first jockey to Peter Thrales stable. If Smirke qualified for the nickname "Cheekie Charlie" it is really rather surprising that no such label was attached to Gethin, for he had little time for the formalities so dear to the hearts of certain owners, who had to accustom themselves to this man's nonchalant air and quick repartee. He once related a story of the time when receiving a telephone call from the titled owner of a horse he had been engaged to ride, he listened to a lengthy tirade from the other end of the line. At the end of this Gethin replied "Yes, certainly my Lord." There was a brief pause, then the deep voice spoke again to say rather testily "This is *Lady* X."

If the British jockeys had viewed Scobie's arrival with any misgivings, or felt it to be incumbent upon them to show this Australian champion a thing or two, these feelings were, for the greater part, soon dispelled by the charm of this man. In the weighing room he proved himself to be an amiable and amusing companion. On the race course they soon found him a formidable and uncompromising opponent. A very hard man to beat and worthy of their respect.

Druids Lodge, near Salisbury, was a stable where some famous coups were hatched in the early part of the century. Scobie, as first jockey to this stable, was to see much of the place, and in his early days there he became something of a commuter, travelling down from Kingston-upon-Thames where he and his family had taken a flat.

Soon he was getting to know the horses and the training gallops on which they worked. Often he would stay overnight in order to ride out with the string at exercise in the dark Winter mornings of the Wiltshire countryside. A regime so different from anything he had experienced in his native Australia. Scobie must often have wished the Druids Lodge had been built on Epsom Downs, the training centre a few miles from his new home, rather than on Salisbury Plain, for he was a home loving man who, for all his affection for horses and racing, was never happier than when he could return home after a busy day and relax with his wife May and daughter Loretta. In this way he felt best able to re-charge himself in order to carry out his many commitments.

It is very desirable that a good rapport should exist between a trainer and his stable jockey. In this Scobie was indeed fortunate, for his "Guv'nor", Noel Cannon, was not only a man with great experience of the Racing world, but also possessed a charm and sweetness of nature which were to remain undiminished by the reversals of fortune in later years. Between 1952 and 1955 he had to contend with the deaths, all more or less unexpected, of three of his leading patrons - Mr. J.V. Rank, Mr. J.A. Dewar and Mr. J. Olding. Added to which his own health was giving cause for concern.

Noel belonged to a distinguished Racing family that originally came from Eton and where, in the first half of the nineteenth century, several members of the family were watermen - one taught the Eton boys swimming and one kept an inn on the Brocas. Noel's father, Joe Cannon, won the Grand National on Regal. Noel himself was commissioned into the Third Hussars on his eighteenth birthday and was subsequently wounded in France.

After the war he trained in India for some time before returning to England to manage a bloodstock agency. When his brother "Boxer" became private trainer to Lady Yule at Balaton Lodge, he took over Bedford Lodge from Boxer and began training there in 1933.

By the time that Scobie arrived at Druids Lodge, Noel Cannon had already been training horses there for fourteen years, ever since Mr. J.V. Rank had installed him there as his private trainer. Like his new stable jockey, Noel was genuinely devoted to horses, and although every trainer of Flat Racing horses hopes for successes in the classics, his deepest affections were for the horses who would remain with him for several years, old geldings like Knights Armour, Black Speck, Strathspey and Highland Division.

In coming to ride in Britain, Scobie had realized a boyhood ambition. Now, with this accomplished, he set his sights on a new goal, to win The Derby. The outstanding disappointment of his career, in Australia, had been his failure to win the most important event in that country's Racing calendar, The Melbourne Cup, a victory that was to elude him for the rest of his life. But that was in the past and Scobie, ever forward-looking and optimistic, now saw the Epsom classic as a more immediate challenge.

However, in The Derby of 1950, neither Scobie nor any of the English horses could ward off yet another triumph for the French, and only one British-bred competitor finished in the leading four that year. Prince Simon, who had suffered such a narrow defeat in The Two Thousand Guineas, started favourite at 2-1. His jockey, Harry Carr, found himself in front much sooner than intended, but felt obliged to go on when Lowrey on Pewter Platter shouted a warning that his mount was beginning to hang and might carry Prince Simon wide at Tattenham Corner. Two furlongs from home the favourite was still going well, but the French challenger Galcador was fast making up ground, and responded in great style when Rae Johnstone asked him for his effort. With a hundred yards to go he led by three-quarters of a length, but was tiring fast. Gamely, Prince Simon came back at him and Galcador held on to win with only a head to spare.

If Scobie was disappointed at taking only fourth place in this race on Telegram II he could at least still look forward to making further attempts to gain this coveted prize. Prince Simon and his connections were less fortunate. In fact it might well seem that this colt had been born under an unlucky star, for having been beaten by a narrow margin in both The Two Thousand Guineas and The Derby, he then ran a good race in The King Edward VII Stakes at Royal Ascot, only to be beaten a head by the 20-1 outsider Babu's Pet. He then went wrong in his preparation for The St. Leger and never raced again. As a stallion he was a total failure and in the end, this horse, who so nearly won both The Guineas and The Derby, was given away as a hack.

At the Brighton meeting in September, Scobie suffered a fall which resulted in the fracture of two small bones in his spine which kept him out of racing for three weeks.

Scobie, ever resilient, was back in the saddle as soon as possible. His first season in British Racing had been a success. The blue and yellow colours of Mr. Rank had entered the winner's enclosure with ever increasing regularity, bringing him up from seventh place in the leading owner's table the previous year, to third place by the end of 1950 Flat Racing season. The leading owner that year was The Aga Khan, with Monsieur M. Boussac the runner up.

In the jockey's table Scobie ended his first season here in sixth place. As everyone had expected Gordon Richards was champion again with two hundred and forty-four winners, topping a double century for the ninth time in his career. Doug Smith was runner up with one hundred and thirty-two and Australian Edgar Britt gained third place with one hundred winners. The leading apprentice that year was Lester Piggott.

1951 was Festival of Britain year, and Racing marked this year of celebrations by devising the King George VI and Queen Elizabeth Festival of Britain Stakes to be run over a mile and a half at Ascot in July. But long before this event took place, Scobie himself had something to celebrate, for this was the year in which he scored his first classic victory on British Turf with Ki Ming in The Two Thousand Guineas. This colt, owned by Chinese restaurateur Mr. Ley On and trained by the Irish ex-jockey Michael Beary, was a large gangling son of Ballyogan out of Ulster Lily. His sire had never won beyond five furlongs and the breeding experts did not give much for Ki Ming's chances over the gruelling Rowley Mile.

But they had reckoned without Scobie, a wizard in the art of nursing horses of doubtful stamina. Waiting until four furlongs from home, he then staked everything on the colt's speed downhill into the Newmarket Dip and opened up such a gap from his nearest rivals that nothing ever looked like catching him. A delighted Scobie brought the big brown colt, already seventeen hands high, back to the winner's enclosure.

After the success of Ki Ming, Mr. Ley On threw a large party in his Soho restaurant and exotic liquor flowed like water. But for Scobie, over indulgence had no appeal. Wisely conscious of the need to keep a clear head, he was a man who liked to celebrate with a glass or two of champagne and enjoyed a good wine with dinner, but bright lights and brash living were not for him. If he indulged himself at all, it was more likely to be with a delicious meal, for Scobie loved his food. In fact, never troubled by weight problems, he could enjoy the kind of meals which most of his fellow jockeys might dream of, but would never dare to eat.

In spite of his victory in The Two Thousand Guineas, Scobie could not be over optimistic about his chances in The Derby that year for Ki Ming's prospects of staying the distance were remote, and when the big test came he was never there with a chance.

The Racing public only remembered him as the colt on which Scobie, by now a great favourite with the race-goers, had won his first classic in Britain. Most of them forgot that he was the son of a sprinter and they almost believed that his jockey was capable of performing miracles. But Scobie, as stable jockey to Noel Cannon, was booked to ride Expeditious who finished in tenth place. Ki Ming, who started favourite, was ridden by T. Gosling.

Arctic Prince was by the French Derby winner Prince Chevalier. He had failed badly when fancied for the Gimcrack Stakes in the previous year and had only reached seventh in The Two Thousand Guineas. But he more than made up for lost time when coming home a winner in The Derby, six lengths ahead of Sybils Nephew, with Signal Box, who finished third, ridden by the great Irish steeplechase jockey Martin Molony. Arctic Prince was trained by W. Stephenson and ridden by Charlie Spares.

Scobie had not felt any very great disappointment at the Derby result, for he knew that his mount lacked the stamina necessary for that race.

He still hoped to partner Ki Ming in races of a more suitable distance.

On the opening day of Royal Ascot, Ki Ming, ridden by Gordon Richards, was beaten into second place in The Queen Anne Stakes by Neron, but returned to Ascot in the Autumn to win the six furlongs Diadem Stakes, this time partnered by Scobie.

Ki Ming's trainer, Michael Beary, came from Tipperary, but the luck of the Irish did not smile on him throughout his career as a jockey and subsequently as a trainer, although he had some notable successes including his win on Mid-day Sun in the 1937 Derby. He served part of his apprenticeship with "Atty" Persse, who believed in old fashioned stable discipline, though whether this worked well in Beary's case is a debatable point. However, Steve Donoghue thought the boy had style and it was on his recommendation that he had his first ride in public.

Donoghue had been right and Beary proved to be not only stylish, but also an effective rider of horses who were difficult to handle. He was also a man of considerable charm, though this did not prevent his making a number of enemies.

He made a fine start to his career as a trainer, but he lacked any financial acumen and soon found himself in serious difficulties. At one point he even took out a jockey's licence again and returned to the saddle in an attempt to recoup some of his losses. It was all in vain and only five years after training Ki Ming to win The Two Thousand Guineas, he died a poor man.

Scobie's first classic victory was followed by success later that year, when at the Newmarket Houghton meeting he won The Cambridgeshire on Fleeting Moment and by the end of the season was beginning to gain recognition as a great artist in the Racing game.

At the end of 1951 the Breasley family returned to Australia and much to the disappointment of Scobie's many supporters in Britain, he spent the following season racing there.

There were sad and unexpected changes at Druids Lodge. Early in 1952 Noel Cannon's chief patron, Mr. J.V. Rank, died suddenly, causing his string to be broken up.

Though now back in Australia, Scobie still felt drawn towards Britain. He had liked British Racing, the horses, the courses and not least of all, the people. In fact he liked everything bar the climate and was prepared to bear even that for the sake of the advantages which England could offer. Not least of these was the education of his daughter, Loretta. He wanted her to have the best that he could provide.

He did not have long to wait. Whisky tycoon, John Dewar, sent his string of racehorses to Druids Lodge and soon Scobie was on his way back to Wiltshire to prepare for the Flat Racing season of 1953.

It was, on the whole, a somewhat uneventful year for Scobie and his connections. He had already stated his intention of retiring after one more year of riding in Britain. But he made that statement before leaving Australia and at that time he had not made the acquaintance of Festoon.

Bred by her owner, Mr. J.A. Dewar, Festoon was a lovely chestnut filly, by Fair Trial out of Monsoon by Umidwar. Monsoon's dam, Heavenly Wind, had been bought as a yearling for only thirty guineas.

Even as a two-year-old Festoon moved so sweetly and held such promise, that Scobie could not resist staying on to ride her in the fillies classics of the following season. And by remaining in this country, he set the seal on a future in which the best was yet to come.

Festoon began her campaign of 1954 by finishing second to Key, ridden by Gordon Richards in The One Thousand Guineas Trial at Kempton Park. Key duly started favourite for The One Thousand Guineas in June. This was Gordon Richards' last ride in a classic race. An accident at Salisbury prevented him from riding in The Derby. But he suffered a far worse accident at Sandown in July, when The Queen's Abergeldie reared up on leaving the paddock, threw her jockey, fell herself and then rolled on him, thus bringing to an end the career of a man who had brought nothing but credit to his profession.

Festoon turned the tables on Key in The One Thousand Guineas. She had been backward at Kempton, but at Newmarket, ridden by Scobie, she made all the running to win as she pleased from Big Berry, with Welsh Fairy third and Key running into fourth place. She failed to stay the distance in The Oaks, but went on to win The Coronation Stakes at Royal Ascot. Her chance of winning her last race, The Sussex Stakes at Goodwood, was ruined by a gale force wind and she finished a long way behind the Queen's colt Landau.

A fortnight after Goodwood, Mr. Dewar died. He had given much to British Racing. Among the winners he bred were The Oaks winner Commotion, the great miler Tudor Minstrel and that excellent sire Fair Trial.

The dispersal sale following Mr. Dewar's death realized a total of three hundred and ninety-eight thousand guineas. Festoon was bought by Mr. Anthony Askew, a nephew of Mr. J.V. Rank, for thirty-six thousand guineas, then a record price in this country for a filly out of training. At stud when mated with Alcide, she produced Atilla, who won over sixteen thousand pounds, in this country as well as The Grosser Preis von Baden. She also bred Pindaric who won the Lingfield Derby Trial, but unfortunately met with a fatal accident in training.

Festoon's performance in The One Thousand

Guineas had delighted Scobie. No longer did he speak of making this his last season as a jockey. But it very nearly was.

Only three days after Festoon's brilliant victory at Newmarket, Scobie lay unconscious on the Alexandra Park turf, left in the wake of thundering hooves after his mount Sayonara slipped and fell five furlongs from home, causing her jockey's head to collide with a heavy post supporting the running rail. Unfortunately there was considerable delay in sending an ambulance to the scene of the accident. The stewards ordered an inquiry into the reason for this negligence, which was blamed on a failure in communications.

Scobie, gravely ill, was rushed to hospital where, for several days, his life hung in the balance and all the Breasley courage and resilience was needed as never before. He won through and weeks later, though still unable to walk or even move his eyes, he was allowed to go home.

The doctors held out little hope that he would ever walk again, much less ride. He was alive. Yet for a normally active man, a sportsman, it was more an existence than a life. Scobie had always been a brave man. He was still brave, but he now sank to a state of profound despair, his sense of balance lost as a result of the accident. What future could any jockey hope for in those circumstances? Scobie's wife gave him all the loving care and encouragement possible. Always there where she was so very much needed bringing an invaluable source of comfort to her stricken husband. But even she could not snatch him back from the depths to which he had sunk. And there he might have stayed.

Fortunately, help came in the form of an old friend who shared Scobie's other great sporting love - golf. Norman von Nida was a volatile little Australian golfer. Here to compete in the Open Golf Championship, he was a man with a will of iron, who made it clear from the start that he would tolerate no arguments. Scobie, who at that time had little heart for much activity, not even his beloved game of golf, was told to "Get up and get out." Into the car went Scobie and his clubs, and it was off to Sunningdale golf course.

Once there, von Nida bullied him mercilessly, while Scobie, still forced to lean on his wife for support, tried to swing a club. Progress was slow, frustrating and sometimes comic; von Nida was unrelenting but within a month his methods, though drastic, proved to be effective, and he knew his friend would ride again.

Von Nida did not win the Open or any golfing title that year, but although he did not know it at the time, he played his part in the winning of four jockey's championships and two Derbys.

# SCOBIE AND SIR GORDON

1956 saw the start of a great partnership. For this was the year that Sir Gordon Richards asked Scobie to ride as first jockey to his stable. Noel Cannon had hoped that he would continue to ride for the Druids Lodge stable, but the offer made by Sir Gordon, estimated to be in the region of five thousand pounds, was too good to be refused. In any case the good rapport and friendship between these two great men of the Turf, made the proposed partnership attractive to both.

Scobie knew of Sir Gordon's achievements in Racing long before coming to Britain, and since joining him on the British Turf had come to know him as a worthy opponent and a close personal friend.

Sir Gordon for his part knew that in Scobie he had found the jockey who, above all others, he wished to retain. He considered him to be one of the most brilliant riders of the era, the undisputed master as a judge of pace and a man on whom he could rely. Years later he said of Scobie "He was a great help to me in my early days as a trainer. I could trust him completely and never raised my glasses to watch him until he was close to home. Then I would know just where to find him. Almost always on the rails, taking the shortest route. I never gave him any riding instructions, he knew what he was doing, and in any case he would not have taken any notice if I had."

Scobie, reared in sunnier climes, did not enjoy the cold Spring mornings of his adopted land. In the early part of the season he rode work only when absolutely necessary, having first taken every precaution to ensure that the experience would be as painless as possible.

His warm chauffeur-driven Rolls, registration SB53, would glide through the chilly countryside on

its way to Sir Gordon's stables.   On arrival chauffeur Bruce would open Scobie's door, remove the
comfortable slippers worn throughout the journey
and carefully fit warm jodhpur boots on to Scobie's
feet.

One March morning after this Cinderella-like
ritual had taken place and Scobie, annointed with a
liberal amount of his favourite after-shave, had
joined Sir Gordon in the middle of the yard, the
big chestnut colt, who until that moment had stood
waiting patiently to be mounted, took one look at
his intended rider, sniffed the air, rolled his eyes
and started towards him on his hind legs.

Sir Gordon, blunt Shropshireman that he could
be, said "You might as well get back in the car
and go home Scobie.   You smell too pretty to ride
work today!"

Scobie and Sir Gordon were different from one
another in many ways.   Scobie lean and long of
limb, Sir Gordon strong, short and stocky.   In temperament too they were dissimilar.   The trainer
known to be calm and placid, with little fluctuation
of mood.   The jockey more unpredictable.   However, for all their differences they had much in
common where horses were concerned, for both
men cared deeply for the animals they rode and
trained.   Added to this, each possessed a natural
rapport with horses.   Sir Gordon's sympathy with
animals was applied in a most sensible and practical way.   When a horse came into training in his
yard, he went to any lengths to understand its
individual needs.   Sometimes a new horse would be
unsettled, off its feed and pacing in its box.
Happily Sir Gordon had devised a way to help such
horses.   In a few of the loose boxes he had cut out
a window in the dividing wall so that the occupant
of one box would be aware of his neighbour in the
next.   Often a steady old gelding would be housed
next to a restless young colt.   This proved very
effective as the restless youngster would soon settle

down when he felt the presence of a friend nearby. As Sir Gordon himself said "They could talk to each other through the window." Undoubtedly he had great feeling for his horses.

The stable at Ogbourne Maisey had high hopes for the 1956 Flat Racing season. The string of almost fifty contained several fashionably bred horses, including some expensive colts bought at the Autumn sales of 1955, who had been allowed to mature, rather than making their debuts before their trainer felt they were ready.

The Hon. Dorothy Wyndham Paget owned more than half the horses in Sir Gordon's yard. She was not only a leading owner, and devoted to her horses, but also one of Racing's more remarkable and eccentric characters.

A daughter of Lord Queenborough, she was also a cousin of Mr. John Hay Whitney, a great supporter of English Racing. By no stretch of the imagination could she have been described as well turned out. Caring nothing for the fripperies of fashion, she invariably appeared in the paddock attired in a long coat that ended just short of her ankles, and a shapeless felt hat. Surrounded by female attendants, she kept the Press at arm's length or even further. Her shyness impelled her to live almost as a recluse at her home in Chalfont St. Giles. She was said to keep unconventional hours, with conferences held far into the night on race courses, long after the last race had been run. She had a will of iron and insisted on having her way. But in spite of her extremely demanding nature, and her undeniable oddness, those who knew her well were genuinely fond of her.

She almost never visited her horses in their training stables, but kept a close check on their progress and loved to have a gamble. The man responsible for placing her bets was her racing adviser, the late Sir Francis Cassel, who had also achieved the distinction of becoming one of Miss

Paget's few male friends. A rare honour, in view of her mistrust of men in general and Racing men in particular!

Perhaps she admired his versatility, for Sir Francis was nothing if not versatile. Apart from being an owner and breeder of racehorses, he was also an accomplished concert pianist.

Once when giving a concert before an audience of seven thousand at The Royal Albert Hall, Sir Francis, resplendent in white tie and tails, retired to his dressing room during the interval, only to be met by a messenger bearing a note containing the following message:- "Give me your tip for the 3.30 at Wolverhampton tomorrow. I must have it right away. D. Paget". The audience, re-assembling to hear the second half of the programme, might have been rather surprised had they known that at that very moment, the distinguished soloist was not, as they may have fondly imagined, preparing himself for some fete of musical expertise, but was in fact looking up a good thing for the 3.30 at Wolverhampton the following day.

None of this would have surprised Scobie or Sir Gordon who were well used to her foibles by that time.

Her first question to Sir Gordon on arrival at the course was invariably "How is the wretched Breasley? Has he got a cold today?" And much to Scobie's amusement, she would say to him "Now Breasley, do not cut it too fine this time," for she knew of her jockey's delight in riding to win by a whisker.

Scobie's first season as jockey to Sir Gordon was a time of mixed fortunes for them both. In the Spring of that year the trainer was involved in an accident which led to a complicated legal action. Then one week before The Two Thousand Guineas, the three-year-old Hamama, who had been bought by former M.P. Mr. John Lewis for around seven thousand pounds, arrived at the Ogbourne stable. On running in The Guineas, he finished a distance last, and pulled up in distress. A heart complaint was suspected and the colt was sent to Newmarket's Equine Research Station, where he underwent extensive electro-cardiac tests, and was taken out of training for the remainder of the season.

To add to Sir Gordon's troubles, five horses owned by Mr. Basil Mavroleon departed from his yard to be sent to Matt Feakes at Lambourn, where their owner already had some horses in training, and stated that he preferred to be the patron of a small stable.

Earlier that year Mavroleon's horse Daemon had won the Burwell Stakes at Newmarket, beating Hugh Lupus, and had started second favourite for The Coronation Cup at Epsom, but finished last behind Tropique. Subsequently it was announced in the Racing Calendar - "The Stewards enquired into the riding of Daemon. After hearing the evidence of the trainer, Sir Gordon Richards, and Breasley, they decided to accept the latter's explanation, but considered he had ridden an injudicious race".

But there were triumphs too for Scobie and his new Guv'nor. Pipe of Peace, owned by Mr. Stavros Niarchos, was rated the best two-year-old of 1956. Before the end of the season, this son of Supreme Court had won races at Salisbury, Goodwood and Newmarket, where he won The Middle Park Stakes by a neck from the French challenger Wayne II, with Military Law a length away third, and Sir Victor Sassoon's handsome colt Crepello fourth.

Pipe of Peace had been bought for seven thousand guineas. He was rather small, but full of quality and headed the colts with nine stone and five pounds in the Free Handicap. Scobie had every reason to hope that his dream of winning The Derby might soon become a reality.

Pipe of Peace wintered well and delighted

Scobie and Sir Gordon by winning the valuable Greenham Stakes at Newbury, his first race' of 1957. Later, in the Two Thousand Guineas, he was third, beaten only half a length and a head by Crepello and Quorum.

For Scobie, anticipation and excitement reached their peak in the days leading up to The Derby. Ever since he could remember, his dearest wish had been to ride to victory in that great race.

Sir Gordon, too, relished the prospect of training a Derby winner, and he had every reason for optimism now there was a potential champion in his yard. But no one knew better than he, just how very elusive a Derby victory can be, for he had been a jockey for thirty-three years before finally achieving his first success in that race though he became champion jockey after only five years in the saddle, and went on to be champion no less than twenty-six times.

1953 was Gordon Richards most glorious year. The year that he became the first member of his profession to receive a knighthood. His private pleasure was intense and shared by the Racing public. Many hoped that he would crown this wonderful achievement with a Derby winner, though not unnaturally loyalties were divided, for this was Coronation Year, and the Queen had a promising entry for the Derby. But a victory for either Sir Gordon's mount Pinza, or Her Majesty's Aureole, would result in boundless jubilation. At the London Press Club lunch, Lord Derby said "Gordon is the first man to have been knighted for his equestrian performances since the Middle Ages. I only hope he is not so much moved that he turns out to ride Pinza in a suit of armour and a lance."

Two days before The Derby, Sir Gordon was second to Ambiguity in the Oaks when riding Kerbeb. The winner was ridden by apprentice Joe Mercer. The big day arrived and Pinza seemed nervous in the paddock, whilst chief rival Aureole was calm. But in the pre-race parade the roles were reversed, with Pinza growing more placid with every passing moment, and Aureole now starting to kick and lash out. Once at the start the horses were quickly away. The early pace was rather slow; Charlie Smirke sent Shikampur into the lead and remained there until reaching the straight. Pinza had moved up into second place with Aureole, Premonition, Mountain King and Good Brandy some three lengths behind him. Coming to the final furlong, Pinza was still full of running and in a dramatic climax to the race, he stormed clear of the field to win by four lengths from Aureole who never got close enough to deliver a challenge. Thus at his twenty-eighth attempt, Gordon Richards won the race that had eluded him for so long. Four years later he was hoping for his first success in The Derby as a trainer. With a top class colt, ridden by Scobie, the jockey who Sir Gordon trusted above all others, he felt there was every chance of this being their year.

Derby Day arrived and Scobie, though confident, felt the excitement of the big occasion. But true professional that he was, he appeared to be calm and in full command of the situation. If he gave any thought to the Noel Murless trained Crepello, he must also have remembered that this colt had been withdrawn from Epsom's Blue Riband Trial Stakes, because the going was thought too firm for him, and the going was again firm for The Derby. Yet in the big race itself, Crepello proved himself capable of coping with the state of the going, by winning by a length from the Irish colt Ballymoss. Once again, as in The Two Thousand Guineas, Scobie, on a fast finishing Pipe of Peace, had to be content with third place. He could not deny that he was disappointed, and felt that Pipe of Peace would certainly have won in an average year. If only this gallant colt had not had the misfortune to be born in the same year as Crepello and Ballymoss, both horses of exceptional calibre, Scobie might well have scored his first Derby success in 1957. Bearing in mind the subsequent fine achievements of Ballymoss, it must be assumed that Crepello was an above average winner of The Derby.

Ballymoss was by the good stallion Mossborough, out of Indian Call. Trained in Ireland by Vincent O'Brian, he was one of the finest horses Scobie ever rode. Following his success at Epsom, he went on to win the Irish Derby. He returned to England for The Great Voltigeur Stakes at York, but on the rather dead ground, he finished only third behind Brioche and Tempest. However, Ballymoss gained another classic victory when winning The St. Leger by a length from Scobie's mount Court Harwell, with Brioche third. It was Vincent O'Brian's first success in an English classic and the first time an Irish horse had ever won The St. Leger. Ridden by jockey T.P. Burns, it was a great day for the Irish.

Scobie's Leger mount, Court Harwell, by Prince Chevalier out of Neutron, had given his trainer Sir Gordon Richards some uneasy moments, being sluggish in his work and slow to come to hand. But this was just the sort of challenge that Scobie enjoyed, and it was largely due to his careful handling that even before running into second place in The Leger, this colt had already won the Bibury Cup at Salisbury on 10th July and three weeks later beat Super Snipe and Preatorian in Goodwood's Warren Stakes. He then won the Oxfordshire Stakes on 17th August at Newbury, and in October beat Alexis and Ommeyad to win the Jockey Club Stakes at Newmarket. Not a bad record for a "sluggish" horse! Sir Gordon always maintained that but for Scobie, it might have been a very different story.

In the same month that Court Harwell triumphed in his race at Newmarket, Sir Gordon

41

and Scobie had a less agreeable experience. While en route for the races, their aircraft was enveloped by a freak cloud of fog, which forced them to land on Bloxwich golf course. "We had a bump or two over the bunkers and in the rough" quipped Sir Gordon. Fortunately no one was hurt and Scobie was able to arrive on Wolverhampton race course in time to ride the winner of the first race. Always a keen golfer, he had to admit that for once, he would rather have given the golf course a miss.

By the end of the season, Scobie had realized an ambition very close to his heart by becoming champion jockey in England for the first time in his career. He had ridden one hundred and seventy three winners, to put him ahead of Edward Hide with one hundred and thirty-one, and Lester Piggott in third place. After eight years of riding in Britain, he was champion at last.

If Ballymoss had robbed Scobie of a St. Leger victory in 1957, he did much to make amends in the following season. In his first outing that year when ridden by his regular jockey, T.P. Burns, he was beaten by the Queen's good four-year-old Doutelle, in the Ormonde Stakes at Chester. However, from then on he never looked back. Ridden by Scobie, he won in succession, The Coronation Cup from the previous year's winner Fric; The Eclipse Stakes by six lengths from Restoration; The King George VI and Queen Elizabeth Stakes at Ascot by three lengths from Almeria with Doutelle, who had beaten him at Chester, in third place. At the end of the 1958 Flat Racing season, Ballymoss was the leading winner with thirty-eight thousand, six hundred and eighty-six pounds from three races in England. He had also run a brilliant race to win The Prix de l'Arc de Triomphe from Fric, coming home through the mud at Longchamp to give Scobie one of the most memorable and prestigious wins of his career.

Having won the richest racing prize in Europe,

Ballymoss should surely have retired at this point, but his American owner wished to send him over for The Washington D.C. International at Laurel, Maryland. This, Scobie's first experience of the American racing scene, did not turn out to be a very happy occasion. Ballymoss was third behind the Englishbred Tudor Era and Sailors Guide. Subsequently the Stewards reversed the placings of the first two. The aftermath of this rough unsatisfactory race left a feeling of sadness and recrimination with the connections of Ballymoss. Scobie was distressed to think that the Racing career of this fine horse, who he had partnered so successfully throughout the season, had ended on a distinctly sour note.

Looking at the lighter side of his American trip, Scobie joked about how they had locked up Britain's champion jockey. For it was the practice in that country for jockeys to be locked in a room on arrival at the course. All riders being required to arrive before the first race, regardless of which race they were engaged to ride in. For reasons of security, a jockey would only be allowed out when it was time for him to ride. Scobie, used to the more easy going and trusting methods adopted by British and Australian Racing, found this practice tiresome, though not without its funny side. But on the whole, he was not enamoured of American Racing at that time.

Court Harwell did not have such a busy year as Ballymoss. He made his debut in April at Newbury; ridden on this occasion by Eph Smith, he was beaten by his old rival Doutelle. With Scobie a month later, he took his revenge when winning The Winston Churchill Stakes at Hurst Park. This time Doutelle had to be content with second place, just ahead of Supreme Courage in third. Before the end of the season Court Harwell retired to stud. Later he sired Meadow Court, winner of the 1965 Irish Sweeps Derby, and also Convamore,

43

runner-up in that race. Meadow Court went on to win The King George and Queen Elizabeth Stakes at Ascot while Convamore won The King Edward VII Stakes. These victories were largely responsible for Court Harwell ending the season as champion sire. By this time he was already at stud in Argentina. The reason for his sale was said to be that during the three years he stood in Ireland, breeders took little interest in him. A rather odd explanation in view of the fact that during those three seasons he covered one hundred and twenty-five mares.

Apart from the outstanding successes of Ballymoss and Court Harwell over the past two seasons, Scobie and Sir Gordon were well pleased with the performance of London Cry, who in 1958, proved to be a "gold mine" for his connections by winning The Craven Stakes at Epsom, other races at Brighton, Salisbury and Newmarket; The Chesterfield Cup at Goodwood and ended the season in a blaze of glory by winning The Cambridgeshire, setting a new weight carrying record for the race with nine stone and five pounds.

Scobie looked back with satisfaction at the 1958 Flat Racing season. Taken all round it had been a good year, and although he did not know it at the time, he had, when riding the winner of the Manton Handicap at Newbury on 24th October, partnered a horse who was to become a great favourite, both with the race-going public and with Scobie himself. The horse was Induna.

One of the most memorable horse and jockey partnerships ever seen on the British Turf, must surely be that of Scobie and Induna. The story of this horse is almost as remarkable as that of Scobie himself.

Foaled in 1953 he was by the grey Migoli who ran second to Pearl Diver in The Derby of 1947. His dam, Solar Princess, was by The St. Leger winner Solario, who created a record in 1932 when sold as a stallion by Tattersalls for forty-seven thousand guineas.

One might suppose that with such a pedigree, this foal would be blessed with good luck from the start. However, the luck that was to follow him in later life was sadly missing at the time of his birth, for his dam died soon after and an alternative means of feeding the young foal had to be found.

Perhaps his luck was already working for him after all, for a Percheron mare had lost her own foal at about the same time that Induna lost his mother. The two were brought together, and the carthorse mare became a foster mother to the little racehorse foal. It was a most successful arrangement.

Induna had his first race as a two-year-old on 29th June 1955. He was unplaced, but less than a month later he came home the 10-1 winner of The Rous Memorial Stakes at Goodwood. Lightly raced that year, he ran once more when unplaced in The Acomb Stakes at York. As a two-year-old and subsequently at three, he was trained by Marcus Marsh at Newmarket and ridden by Charlie Smirke.

At three he won The Derby Trial Stakes at Lingfield beating Scobie's mount Pearl Orama into second place. In the Derby, won by the French colt Lavandin, he could only reach tenth place.

As a four-year-old he went to Druids Lodge to be trained by Noel Cannon. Now ridden by Scobie's fellow countryman Jack Purtell, Induna had a busy season, but did not win a race until September, when he won The Great Yorkshire Handicap at Doncaster. He soon followed this victory with yet another when beating Chantry in The Purley Stakes at Lingfield.

In 1958, after having won The Claremont Stakes at Sandown in April and being placed in four other races, he teamed up with Scobie for the first time and won The Manton Handicap at Newbury from Big Pearl and Vantage on 24th October.

1959 was a great year for Scobie and Induna who, now trained by Sir Gordon Richards, was never out of the frame in any of his races that year. They won The Claremont Stakes at Sandown, which Induna had also won the previous year, The Hwfa Williams Handicap over the same course, The August Welter Stakes at Brighton and The Gordon Carter Handicap at Ascot in September. Added to which he was placed in several other races during the year and walked over in The Poulson Stakes at Sandown.

1960 found Induna competing in no less than thirteen races, of which he won five and was only twice unplaced. The rapport between this horse and Scobie was something rare, each seemed to have a complete understanding of the other. They became great favourites with the race-going public and went on happily together winning several more races until Sir Gordon decided to retire Induna at the age of ten. He had taken part in sixty-four races and his trainer felt it was time to send him back to his owner Sir Reginald Macdonald-Buchanan and a quiet life.

That might have been the end of his story had Induna not been the horse he was. Soon after his arrival, it was obvious that all was not well. He was unsettled, paced nervously in his box and re-fused to eat. It was felt that, given time, he would settle into his new environment, but as time went by his condition deteriorated.

Sir Reginald, deeply worried about his horse, contacted the one man who knew Induna better than anyone else - Sir Gordon Richards.

The trainer was quick to realise the cause of the trouble and asked for Induna to be returned to Whitsbury as quickly as possible. And once back in his familiar surroundings, out on the gallops with the other horses, he soon became his old self. Sir Gordon understood horses and was perceptive enough to realize that Induna had been involved in the

Racing scene for so long, that without the stimulus of the only way of life he had ever known, the horse pined and fretted.

An unusually sensitive and intelligent horse, he was soon happy again and full of his own importance as he acted as "school master" to the young horses. A real "character", he remained Sir Gordon's hack for the rest of his life. Then, as a final tribute, he was buried on the top of the hill at Whitsbury. A most suitable resting place for this horse who loved racing.

# THE MAGICAL HAT TRICK

The 1961 Flat Racing season opened at Lincoln in March. As always the excitement was almost tangible on this day so eagerly awaited throughout the long Winter days. The first day of the Flat is very special to the true Racing enthusiast, for the season lies before us like a blank sheet of paper on which anything may be written, and almost anything is possible.

Yet not every surprise will be pleasant and for Scobie, tanned, relaxed and newly returned from holidays, a surprise - perhaps more of a shock - was not long in presenting itself. On March 22nd Blue Palm reared up at the start putting Scobie on the ground and then falling on him. X-rays showed a broken collar-bone and a broken toe. This along with a sprained right shoulder and extensive bruising kept Scobie out of the saddle for almost a month. But ever resilient, he was back by April 18th to win The Bunbury Stakes at Epsom on Conspirator, who was backed down to the unlucrative price of 7-1 on.

Taken all round it was a lean start to a year that would ultimately prove to be very successful for Scobie and his connections. At the first Spring meeting at Newmarket he did not ride a single winner, but came back in great form on May 10th at Bath with four winners - Bianca, Miss Bahamas, Master Lou and Messua - and then went on to win The Empire Handicap the following day on his old friend Induna.

This was not to be a year of classic successes for Scobie and although he rode several winners during the Epsom Derby Meeting, he was unplaced on both his Derby mount, Nicomedus, and on Indian Melody in the Oaks.

Scobie was not alone in suffering disappointment in the Derby, but had little to complain about when compared to the unfortunate anti-post backers of Sir Victor Sassoon's - Pinturischio. This Pinza colt, trained by Noel Murless, had not run as a two year-old, but had acquired a good reputation at Newmarket and duly won The Wood Ditton Stakes at three. He started favourite for The Two Thousand Guineas at 7-4 and finished fourth behind Rockavon. This performance satisfied his connections and ante-post money poured on him for The Derby.

Yet he still faced one engagement before the Epsom classic, as it was intended to run him in The Dante Stakes at York on May 16th, but on the day before that race, while still in his box at home, Pinturischio was "got at" by a doping gang and was unable to run. A strong colt, he recovered well from the attack and his trainer felt that he would be able to take the field in The Derby. However, this was not to be, for whoever was responsible left nothing to chance when perpetuating a second attack on the unfortunate animal, the severity of which was such as to prevent him ever racing again.

In 1961 the methods of analysis were less sophisticated than they are today in the nineteen-eighties. A great many tests are taken each year and almost all of these are negative. As the cost of these tests is very high, many hold the opinion that the money could be put to better use. But perpetual vigilance must continue if we are to keep Racing as a sport and not as a profitable market for unscrupulous criminals.

In the same year as the doping of Pinturischio, an even more senseless attack was made on another horse. This took place in July when Pandofell, winner of The Gold Cup and due to run in The Sunninghill Park Stakes at the Ascot July Meeting, was found dazed and ill on the morning of the race. Hardly able to stand and with his eyes badly cut, he was naturally unable to race that day. His trainer, F. Maxwell, was shocked and tests were taken which proved that the horse had been given phenobarbitone. No one profited from this crime as there was no anti-post betting on the race.

These were the days when doping gangs often had things far too much their own way. They indiscriminately attacked helpless animals, endangered the livelihood of trainers and brought the sport of horse racing into severe disrepute.

On May 4th 1961, the Duke of Norfolk's Committee, formed to enquire into the question of doping, published its report. This brought about the abolishment of the unjust rule whereby the trainer of any horse found to have been doped was automatically disqualified from holding a trainer's licence. The amendment read:

> Where any horse has run in any race under these Rules and has been found on examination under Rule 14 (VI), to have received any amount of any substance (other than a normal nutrient), being a substance which by its nature could affect the racing performance of a horse, the trainer of the horse in question shall be fined not less than £100 and, at the discretion of the Stewards of the Jockey Club, his Licence or permit may be withdrawn. However, the Stewards may waive the fine if they are satisfied that the substance was administered unknowingly and that the trainer had taken all reasonable precautions to avoid a breach of this Rule.

This rule, fairer to trainers and giving the stewards more room to manoeuvre, was very well received.

Scobie himself was all in favour of any action brought about for the benefit of racing. He had nothing but contempt for anyone willing to injure a horse. That they should do so for financial gain was almost unbelievable to this man known for his gentle rapport with animals. Yet as with all

Racing men, Scobie had to face the fact that such people existed in the sport he loved, and along with everyone else involved with horseracing, he had to remain constantly on guard against them.

It was in 1961 that Scobie felt himself to be unjustly treated by a certain section of the Press, who, he considered to have implied that he was riding for the benefit of the bookmaker, although the reporters concerned strongly denied that they had suggested any such thing.

By now Scobie was a firm favourite with the Racing public, though a visit to any betting shop might have given quite a different impression. Once inside any one of these establishments the visitor would hear Scobie described as anything from a devil to an angel. One moment he would be the greatest jockey ever to get astride a horse, and a moment later he would emerge as a man whose parentage was being sadly called into question. None of this meant anything at all to Scobie who would have been the first to laugh it off. Only when adverse and unfair criticism appeared in print was it likely to annoy this usually easy going man.

If this was not a year for classic victories, it was nevertheless a most successful year, for Scobie was a frequent visitor to the winner's enclosure as winner after winner came home for him - three or four in an afternoon, being in no way unusual. It was the year that he rode the three-year-old Skymaster to victory in races at Sandown and Salisbury and on July 25th brought him in the good priced winner of The Stewards Cup at Goodwood at 100-7 when beating Deer Leap and Klondyke Bill. Skymaster was later to sire the great sprinter Be Friendly who Scobie counted one of the fastest horses he ever rode.

He also rode good priced winners at Royal Ascot with Thames Trader in The Bessborough Stakes and Futurama in The Ribblesdale Stakes. He scored a hat trick at Brighton on August 9th when winning on Bigigi, Snuff Box and Hot Springs.

By now he was leading jockey at many courses, and although his career had gone from strength to strength he still longed for victory in one of the classic races which had eluded him throughout his eleven years of riding in Britain - The St. Leger. The last classic race of the Flat Racing season and run at one of his best loved courses - Doncaster.

His mount in the 1961 St. Leger - Just Great - had already served him well earlier in the season when living up to its name by winning several races including The Great Voltigeur Stakes at York on August 23rd.

Sadly for Scobie, Just Great came nowhere in The St. Leger and, in fact, he was destined never to ride the winner of this coveted classic. Apart from failing to score in the race he had so longed to win, Scobie excelled himself at the Doncaster September meeting for he won races on Tudor Period, Alanix, Vendeuse, Thames Trader and the aptly named Will Reward.

He ended in fine style by landing a treble on the last day of the Flat with wins on Dario, Chesterfields Advice and then the last race of the season, The Grange Handicap on Middle Watch.

By the end of the year he was Champion Jockey for the second time having ridden one hundred and seventy-one winners. Lester Piggott, the previous year's champion, finished in second place with one hundred and sixty-four winners and Doug Smith third with one hundred and forty-four.

1962 brought a decline in race-course attendances. Betting shops spread in rich profusion all over the country and television often covered three meetings on a Saturday so that many former patrons of the cheaper enclosures were happier watching from the comfort of their own homes, rather than enduring the inadequate facilities offered by many courses. The situation was not improved when Hurst Park, a popular and handy spot for Londoners, fell a prey to property developers, thus vanishing from the fixture list for ever.

Scobie had no mount in either The Two Thousand Guineas or The One Thousand Guineas in 1962. In The Derby he rode the previously unraced Prince d'Armour who was kicked at the start, was never near to the leaders and finished in sixth place. This bay colt must have had one of the shortest careers ever known in racing, for after this brief introduction to the race-course, he never raced again.

The Derby this year proved to be one of the most sensational in the history of the race. Of the twenty-six runners, seven fell when running down to Tattenham Corner. The fallers included the favourite Hethersett. On reflection it would appear that too many mediocre competitors were entered for the race, as a result, when these colts were beginning to drop back, the better ones were striving to improve their position. With over twenty horses galloping flat out downhill, jostling and crowding almost inevitably took place. Romulus, one of the first to fall, brought down the favourite. Larkspur just managed to pull away from the rails to keep on his feet. But Crosson, Pendaric, Persian Fantasy, Changing Times and King Canute II all came down. The latter broke a leg and had to be destroyed. Of the seven jockeys involved only Bobby Elliott did not need hospital treatment. Harry Carr could not ride again before the end of July and Stan Smith was out for even longer.

Having avoided disaster, Larkspur ran on like a true stayer winning by two lengths from the French colt Arcor, with another French competitor, Le Cantilien, third. The winner was owned by Mr. Raymond Guest, for some years United States Ambassador to Ireland. Trained by Vincent O'Brien and ridden by the Australian jockey Neville Sellwood, Larkspur, who was by the 1954 Derby winner Never Say Die, was far from being a great classic colt. The remainder of his racing career was undistinguished. He was certainly not in the same class as Sir Ivor who won for Mr. Guest in 1968. This fortunate owner also won two Cheltenham Gold Cups and The Grand National with L'Escargot.

In the Autumn of 1962 Larkspur's jockey, Neville Sellwood, was killed when riding the inappropriately named Lucky Seven at Maisons-Laffitte. A sad blow to the Racing world.

Vincent O'Brien had hoped that his charge might complete a double by winning at The Curragh in the first running of the Irish Sweeps Derby. Scobie was engaged to ride Larkspur in this race and duly started favourite at 9-4. But victory went to the French colt Tambourine II, trained by Pollet and ridden by Roger Poincelet, in a thrilling finish they won by a short head from Arctic Storm, with Sebring five lengths away in third place. Although Scobie was making good headway on Larkspur four furlongs out, the colt was clearly outclassed and could only finish fourth.

At Royal Ascot Scobie achieved a superb double with Mrs. L. Carver's six-year-old gelding - Trelawny, who had won The Chester Cup two years previously. On the opening day of the meeting, they won The Ascot Stakes with nine stone and eight pounds and only three days later The Queen Alexandra Stakes with nine stone and five pounds.

At this time Trelawny was trained by George Todd and a very fruitful association this proved to be. But it was to another trainer that the gelding owed much of his success and even his life. At four, the year he won The Chester Cup, he was trained by Syd Mercer and seemed to be improving after being slow to develop as a three-year-old. But in The Goodwood Stakes he broke a cannon bone. Mercer jumped into a car with two racecourse vets and sped down the course to the injured animal. The vets examined the leg and declared that there was no chance of saving the horse. It might well have been the all too familiar story of a racehorse with a broken bone being put down then and there at the scene of the accident.

Happily for Trelawny, he had in his trainer a horse doctor extraordinary and Mercer refused to agree to the vets recommendation that the horse be put down. He took Trelawny home and put plaster on the break. For many days his patient could put no weight on one side, but the skilled attention he received succeeded in getting the broken bone to mend. Putting his hand under the hoof eighteen days later, Syd could feel the horse holding back his weight from the injured leg. He tried again on the following day and this time felt just the lightest pressure. Four days later he had to snatch his hand away. The plaster was removed and Trelawny went on to win another sixteen thousand pounds in prize money. This son of Black Tarquin lived to become one of the most popular horses in the country. He provided Scobie with some of his most memorable victories and was given a reception at Goodwood the following year that was reminiscent of the days of Brown Jack.

Syd Mercer's extra-ordinary ability to cure sick horses baffled vets and trainers alike. Born into a farming family, he was on horseback almost before he could walk. During the First World War he was offered, and accepted, the Remount Officer's job of buying and handling thousands of horses for the Army. During this time he gained the practical knowledge which was to make him into a walking encyclopedia of equine cures, who, with no professional qualifications, often succeeded where the qualified vets had failed. He never divulged the secret of his "magical horse powers" although they were known to contain herbs picked from the hedgerows.

Syd Mercer went on to become a powerful

force as a trainer, first at Rugeley in Staffordshire and later at Newmarket, Knowle and finally Lambourn.

A raconteur with a wry wit. When his horse Weepers Boy won the Senior Services Gold Cup at York, he collected sixteen thousand pounds in winnings. After the race, Peter O'Sullevan wrote "I'll go to the workhouse proclaiming that Weepers Boy's place in the winner's enclosure should have been taken by High Flying, who walked out of the stalls, but was flying at the finish."

Meeting O'Sullevan at Newbury a fortnight later, Mercer said "I read your write-up Peter, it was fine, but you needn't go to the workhouse, there's an old people's home in Woodstock. I went to see if I could get you in but it was full of your bloody punters!" Unfortunately, the urbane Mr. O'Sullevan's reply is not known.

1962 went on with Scobie notching up victories at courses all over the country. August arrived and uppermost in Scobie's mind was his ever increasing longing to win The St. Leger. At the beginning of the month, The Vaux Gold Tankard at Redcar was won by Monterrico, who on 6th July at Sandown had won The Commonwealth Stakes. This colt was to be Scobie's mount in The Leger that year.

Monterrico was nothing if not well bred. By Alycidon out of Timid Tilly by Rockefella and with the great Hyperion as a great grand-parent on both sides of his pedigree, he might well have been expected to emulate his illustrious ancestors. Moreover he had cost fourteen and a half thousand guineas as a yearling. Not an inconsiderable sum of money in 1960. He was a late developer and in any case his early races had not been far enough to show him to the best advantage; furthermore, as with so many of Alycidon's progeny, his temperament was rather unreliable. When winning The Vaux Gold Tankard he had done much to enhance his reputation, for although he was last to leave the gate, he recovered quickly, challenged two furlongs out, and in a driving finish got up to win by a short head from Sostenuto, who went on to win The Ebor Handicap by eight lengths.  Monterrico was entered for one more race before The Leger; The Great Voltigeur Stakes at the York August meeting. In this race he met with serious interference which caused him to drop back, yet even then, after rounding the turn he fought back and put in such a strong run that he looked like catching Hethersett and Miralgo in the last furlong; however, he lost ground and finished three lengths behind the first two.

Weighing up his colt's chances of winning The Leger, Scobie felt optimistic.  Without interference the colt might have won his last race.  He had won The Vaux Gold Tankard in fine style, he stayed well and could act in any going.  Perhaps this would be the year for Scobie's first Leger victory. It was a race he would have dearly loved to win and along with The Derby and The Oaks was a classic race which had so far eluded him.

Sometimes Scobie wondered why he gave in to this annual ritual of hoping, dreaming, checking the form of the other runners and following any report of their progress with interest.  Yet the endless weighing up of his chances during the weeks before an important race had become an inescapable part of his life.  Sometimes he wanted to believe that the ultimate result would be whatever fate decreed it would be and all he could do was to handle the race as best he could.  Yet for all that he could not switch himself off from the excitement, anticipation and hope that always filled his thoughts before he was due to ride in a classic race.

On the Saturday before The St. Leger, his optimism was dealt a nasty blow.  During a training session, Monterrico refused to gallop, behaved temperamentally and went off his feed for several days.

The day of the big race arrived. Scobie appeared calm and cool. Standing in the Doncaster Parade Ring with the trainer, Harry Wragg, he looked as nonchalant as ever. Yet although Monterrico had reverted to one of his more amenable moods, his jockey knew only too well that the colt's recent transgressions might have taken their toll. But in the race Monterrico proved to be in splendid form and ran an excellent race, even reversing the York placings with Miralgo. It was so very near to being Scobie's first Leger victory, but the field contained the brilliant colt Hethersett, and in the end this son of Hugh Lupus showed his superiority with an easy four length victory from Monterrico and Miralgo.

Scobie was naturally disappointed, but not really surprised. He had been in Racing far too long to be surprised at the outcome of any race. There would be another chance in the years ahead and only time would tell what the future St. Legers would bring his way.

As for Monterrico. He did not live up to the expectation that he might make a top class stayer. Some Racing men claim that it is unlucky to change a horse's name, and Monterrico started his racing career as Aldon Rock. But maybe it is only a coincidence that luck seemed to desert him after his creditable performance in The St. Leger of 1962.

The Newmarket Houghton meeting which took place just over a month after The Leger, saw Scobie in great form. On the opening day he scored a hat trick with victories in The Rous Memorial Stakes with Queens Hussar, who was later to become the sire of the great Brigadier Gerard; The Suffolk Nursery Handicap on Tarara, and then won The Rutland Handicap with Harvest Melody.

On the second day of the meeting, a massive field of forty-six runners lined up for The Cambridgeshire. Scobie's mount in this prestigious race

Brighton 3rd August 1966. Hearty congratulations from Scobie as Norah Wilmot becomes the first woman to officially train a winner under Jockey Club rules.

A second Derby winner for Scobie as Lady Zia Wernher's 'Charlottown' comes home ahead of 'Pretendre' and 'Black Prince' in 1966.

12th February 1950. The Breasleys set foot on English soil for the first time after disembarking from the liner "Stratheden".

In 1961 a young 'rider' gets advice from a champion.

Scobie's favourite racehorse, the great 'Ballymoss'.

'Trelawny' is led in after winning The Ascot Stakes of 1962. Three days later he won The Queen Alexandra Stakes at the same meeting.

Seven-year-old Induna winning Hurst Park's George Lambton Cup.

'London Cry' who won the Cambridgeshire Stakes at Newmarket on 29th October 1958.

'Ki Ming' the giant colt who gave Scobie his first classic victory in England when they won the 1951 Two Thousand Guineas.

The lovely chestnut filly 'Festoon' winning the 1954 One Thousand Guineas from 'Big Berry' and 'Welsh Fairy'. Scobie's second classic victory in this country.

The 1964 Derby winner 'Santa Claus' is led into the winners enclosure having made his jockey a happy man by giving him his first Derby victory at the age of fifty.

Seen here with daughter Loretta and grand-daughter Zonda. Scobie and May celebrated twenty-seven years of marriage on 5th November 1962.

Scobie talking to singer Bing Crosby, a part owner of Derby entrant 'Dominion Day', whilst watching gallops at Epsom before the colts classic of 1967.

Another Bing - Scobie's Alsatian pet named after
the American singer.

"Can't let him catch a cold". It looks as though the attendant ·may have put his money on Scobie, who was about to ride the winner of the 1966 Derby - 'Charlottown'.

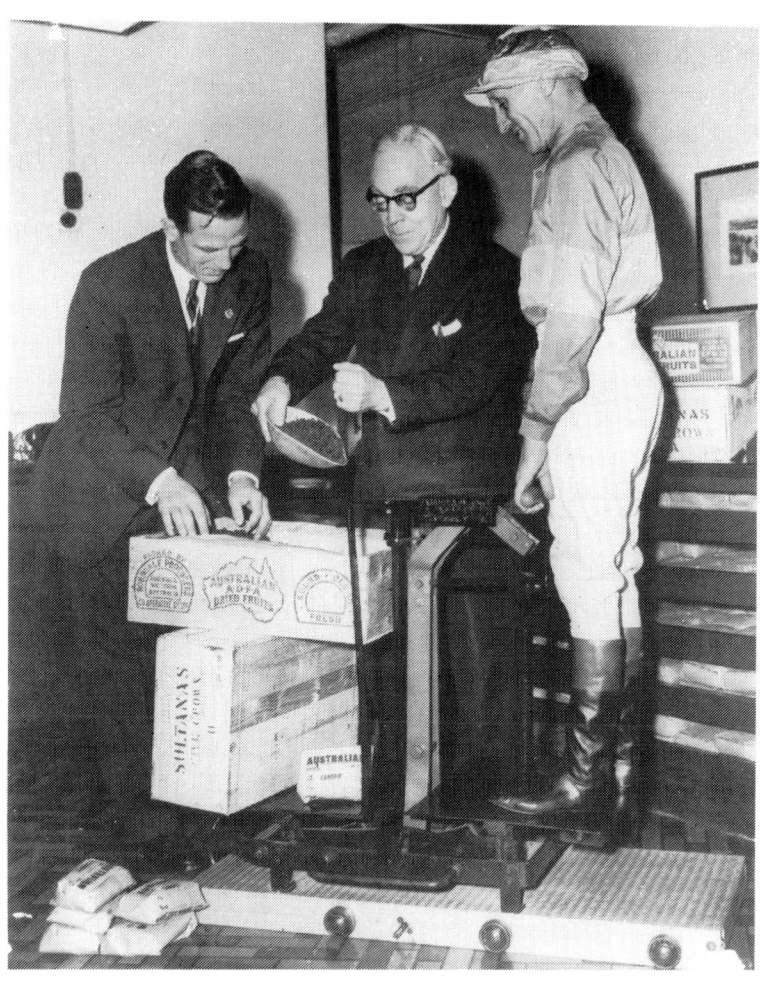

To celebrate 1,000 winners in Europe, Scobie was weighed against his own weight in Australian sultanas, which were later distributed to children's hospitals.

Joe Mercer in hospital after a fall at Folkstone in 1967, receives a visit from fellow jockeys Scobie Breasley and Jimmy Lindley.

A sparkling performance gets a suitable reward. A double magnum was presented to Scobie at Royal Windsor races after he had ridden his 2,000th winner in this country.

# 1967
## A wonderful year for 'Be Friendly'.

Off to a good start by winning The Two Thousand Guineas Trial at Kempton.

The Kings Stand Stakes at Royal Ascot.

Then – as a crowning achievement he beats 'Mountain Call' by a neck to win the Vernons November Sprint Cup at Haydock Park.

was that game, consistant filly Hidden Meaning, who had recently come home the winner of The Swinley Forest Handicap at Ascot, where she passed the post six lengths ahead of her nearest rival Zaragoza who was receiving twenty-one pounds from the winner. On that occasion she had defeated the sixteen other contenders with ease. Now in The Cambridgeshire she found no difficulty in showing the other forty-five runners a clean pair of heels. In fact so impressive was her victory, that one Sunday newspaper was quoted as saying "On Wednesday afternoon last, at around 3.12, a solitary horseman was seen wending his way across Newmarket Heath". This conveys the ease with which she won, easing up towards the finish, to pass the post two lengths and a short head in front of Hasty Cloud and Bewildroom. Scobie was delighted with the filly, all the more so as he had now completed a double in the Cambridgeshire; his other victory being with Fleeting Moment in 1951.

On the third day Scobie rounded off a very successful meeting with an easy win on John Cameron in The Prendergast Stakes.

Scobie liked Newmarket, and because of his fine judgement of pace, he always excelled on the straight Rowley Mile.

November came and with it the end of the 1962 Flat Racing season. Scobie was champion jockey again with his best ever total of one hundred and seventy-nine. Doug Smith was in second place with one hundred and twenty-seven and fellow Australian, Ron Hutchinson, just scraped into third place with ninety-seven, only one ahead of Lester Piggott with ninety-six winners to his credit.

Scobie had enjoyed a most successful season. Yet he could be self-critical and his ever driving ambition caused him to feel some regret that another season had passed in which a victory in The Derby, The Oaks and The St. Leger had eluded him yet again. His best score ever in the jockey's table did not wholly console him in his regret at having failed to reach his personal target of two hundred winners.

This way of thinking was typical of Scobie, who could be very hard on himself at times. Where another man might have been content with so much success, he always the perfectionist, never gave way to complacency. It was an attitude of mind which served him well, for it drove him on at the very point where others might have rested on their laurels.

Now with another Racing season behind him, he turned his thoughts towards a holiday in the sun. A time for family, friends and relaxation. Although Scobie's ideas of relaxation might have exhausted a lesser man, consisting as they did of a seemingly unending round of feverish activity. Fortunately he possessed all the physical and nervous energy necessary for his extensive programme of leisure activities, which usually included plenty of water-ski-ing, swimming, tennis and as many parties as he could give for his friends. Yet he would always return at the start of the next Flat Racing season, tanned, relaxed and raring to go.

1963 proved to be another bad year for English trained horses. The one English classic success was in The Two Thousand Guineas when Only for Life, ridden by Jimmy Lindley, beat Ionian by a short head with Corpora three lengths away in third place. Challengers from abroad also won The Coronation Cup, The Eclipse Stakes, The King George VI and Queen Elizabeth Stakes and The Champion Stakes.

For Scobie too the year was to bring more than a fair share of problems. With only three days to go to the opening meeting of the Flat Racing season, Scobie's daughter, Loretta, and son-in-law, Brian Swift, were taken to hospital after their return from a holiday in a Swiss ski resort. They were found to be suffering from typhoid.

Always the true professional, Scobie never allowed his emotions to interfere with his riding commitments. But it was not easy, in times of stress, to maintain the high standards which, by now, were always expected of him. That he was able to do this says much for his dedication and sense of duty to hi retainers and to the owners who relied upon him to enhance the chances of any horse he was riding. Happily, Loretta and Brian made a good recovery and Scobie, who cared deeply for his only child, felt a profound sense of relief.

At Ogbourne too, a feeling of uncertainty prevailed. For seven years Sir Gordon as tenant, and Norah Laye as landlord, had enjoyed a peaceful relationship, apart from a few minor altercations there had been no serious differences between them. But for some time Mrs. Laye, now elderly and rather eccentric, had expressed a wish to regain possession. Finally she agreed that the tenancy should continue for one more year, so Sir Gordon faced the 1963 season with confidence, but with the anxiety of having to find new premises in time for the start of the following season. Backed financially by Michael Sobell and his son-in-law Arnold Weinstock, Sir Gordon was instructed by them to buy the entire establishment at Ogbourne, regardless of price, but Norah Laye would not contemplate such a proposal. There was a chance that George Todd would sell Manton, but stumbling blocks of one kind or another prevented a sale being made. It was a worrying time. However, negotiations for a lease on the Whitsbury stables, owned by William Hill, appeared to be bearing fruit and were completed before the end of a season which brought Sir Gordon no significant success on the race course. It was also the year when Scobie and his guv'nor realised that for their old friend, Induna, racing days were coming to an end. He had served them well, but on 3rd June at Chepstow he ran his last race coming second to Crowded

Room in The Severn Salmon Handicap.

1963 was also the year when Scobie's libel actions against Odhams Press and two racing journalists, Tom Nickalls and Don Cox, were heard in The Queen's Bench Division of The High Court of Justice. A stressful time for everyone concerned, but more of this later.

If this looked to Scobie like a year when nothing would go right, he could console himself with the fact that at least on the Racing scene, good fortune smiled upon him. Not that classic successes came his way this year, for they were all too elusive, and he might well have been forgiven for thinking that his ambition to ride a Derby winner might never be realized. His mount in the Epsom colt's classic, Fern, was never near the leaders. Victory went to the French with M. Dupre's Relko, partnered by Yves Saint-Martin, who won by six lengths from Merchant Venturer, with Ragusa third.

Thirteen years had passed since Scobie had arrived in England with the intention of riding for just one more year. Now he no longer spoke of retirement as he looked forward to setting himself new goals. Always aiming for something new, he was, at nearly fifty years of age, like a man who, by some magical powers, had reversed the ageing process. His critics speculated as to how long he would be able to remain at the top of his profession. It was to be longer than they thought.

With the first three classics of the season over, Scobie was soon turning his thoughts towards Royal Ascot. He had, of course, brought off a spectacular double the previous year when Trelawny won both The Ascot Stakes and The Queen Alexandra Stakes at the corresponding meeting, and to the delight of everyone, they did it again. This time with seven-year-old Trelawny carrying ten stone in The Ascot Stakes and conceding no less than forty-nine pounds to runner-up Sea Leopard. Three days later they came home easy winners of The Queen Alexandra Stakes, thus achieving the same double once again. Trelawny knew all about racing by now and appeared to relish the tremendous reception he was given upon entering the winner's enclosure.

Just over one month later, he won The Goodwood Cup with ease. The other contenders could not get near to him. He made all the running over the two mile five furlongs of the race and came in to a hero's welcome. Undoubtedly the most popular horse in England at that time. Scobie was delighted. He had already started the meeting with a treble on the first day, when he won The Craven Stakes on Aboukir; The Warren Stakes on In The Gloaming and The New Ham Stakes with Port Merion. On the second day he rode the winner of The King George Stakes, Secret Step. Now it looked as though his victory on Trelawny would give him a double on the third day for he had already ridden the winner of The Rous Memorial Stakes, Roan Rocket. But in fact he was able to go one better, for he then rode Tiger to victory in The Gordon Stakes, the race following The Goodwood Cup, thereby scoring not a double, but a treble. Scobie could look back on The Goodwood July Meeting of 1963 and think that it had truly lived up to the name - "Glorious Goodwood".

By this time Scobie had established himself so firmly in the affections of his supporters that, for them, he had become a true symbol of all that was best in British Racing. Few ever remembered that he had come thousands of miles in order to ride in this country. He was one of them, and they were proud of him. This was gratifying for Scobie, although if some of the Racing public had forgotten his origins, he never did. Keenly interested in the affairs of his homeland, Australia, he followed closely all her events of either a sporting or political nature. He still had many relations in the country of his birth, was planning to spend his holiday there the following year, and perhaps make a final attempt to win the elusive Melbourne Cup. Australia was still home to Scobie in 1963. But England was home too and in the years to come it would be to this country that Scobie and his wife would return after several years of training horses in France and America. And this time, setting foot on English soil after a long absence, Scobie could only say "Its wonderful to be home." The adoption was complete.

But in 1963, Scobie was still very much a man of two countries and learning something new about the British Racing scene with every passing day. It had much to offer him, often in ways not immediately apparent. Scobie had been born into racing; his early days had been spent with horses and his career as a jockey had been an almost foregone conclusion. It was a good start, and might have seemed the ideal beginning. On the other hand, he had been denied the wonder of discovering racing for the first time at an age when he could appreciate the true magnetism of the sport. Happily British Racing brought fresh aspects to a seemingly familiar scene.

Scobie knew from the start that racing in Britain involved an almost constant change of location. With racecourses scattered all over the country, mostly staging two-day meetings, he was constantly on the move. He had been prepared for this, so it came as no surprise. What he could not have anticipated was the intrigueing change of atmosphere which manifested itself as the Racing world moved from one racecourse to another. It was a world populated by the familiar faces of owners, trainers, fellow jockeys, the Racing Press and the many others who frequented the Racing scene. They took on the familiarity of a family, with all the rivalries, loves, hates and intrigues of families the world over.

The people were the same, yet each course

was unique, each stamped with a definite character of its own. At Newmarket, the headquarters of Flat Racing, the visitor is confronted with what at first appears to be a vast green desert, where the approach to Racing is at once businesslike and sporting. High up in the spartan buildings, gazing out over seemingly endless heath, one might be forgiven for allowing full rein to the imagination as an almost tangible presence of horses of long ago becomes an all pervading force and we have to draw ourselves back to the present time, to the racehorses of today, so soon to add their names to Racing records dating from the seventeeth century. This is Newmarket, cold and austere; powerful and committed.

To visit Goodwood is to enter a different world. Set in the soft undulating Sussex countryside, "Glorious Goodwood" casts its own particular spell. Staging some of the most prestigious events in the Racing Calendar, it attracts some of the best horses in Britain and Europe. Yet along with the serious Racing interests, a certain frivolity prevails. The July Meeting is still a social event. The fashions, though less formal, can compare favourably with anything Royal Ascot may have to offer. The champagne flows and, when the sun shines, this charming racecourse with its garden party atmosphere, is suffused in a golden glow.

At Ascot, and at the Royal Meeting in particular, grandeur is the order of the day. Everything is presented on a larger scale than at any other racecourse, with the prestige, prize money and often the ladies' hats aiming to be bigger and better than ever before. The one mile Royal Hunt Cup Course stretches down to The Golden Gates, through which the carriages of the royal party pass at the start of Her Majesty The Queen's drive down the course, to be viewed by a crowd of several thousands, packed on to stands which seem to go on for as far as the eye can see. A winner at this meeting is the ambition of almost every owner and the trainers who have spent months preparing their charges with this in mind. Royal Ascot is also the occasion where Racing is "at home" to the outside world; opening its gates to the uninitiated, who flock to the carefully tended green lawns, not so much through an overwhelming interest in the prowess of the thoroughbred, as from a desire to see and be seen at Racing's smartest social occasion. And although some believe that the fashions detract from the horses, Royal Ascot continues to stage splendid racing in an equally splendid setting.

The smaller courses also have their own particular charm. Who, having been to Windsor on a Summer's day could fail to appreciate the beauty of the willow trees, forming a perfectly hung curtain of soft green against a clear blue sky?

At Sandown Park the landscaping of the surrounding area, the beauty of the flower beds and velvety lawns create a flawless setting for some exciting and competitive events.

Kempton Park lying in three hundred acres of parkland that were mentioned in the Domesday Book, is compact. Its programme may be somewhat unimaginative, but efforts are being made to put this right. Not a grandiose course, more the bread and butter of Racing, yet with an undeniable homeliness and charm. It certainly involves less walking for the spectator than is the case at Epsom, the home of The Derby, where the Parade Ring is so far from the Stands that the jockeys are taken by car to join their mounts. The Derby meeting is an occasion to delight the extrovert - noisy, boisterous and scarcely warranting the morning dress, de rigueur for Derby Day itself. Yet for all its shortcomings, Epsom on this day has a heart as big as the surrounding downlands.

Nor are racecourses of character and splendour confined to the South and over the years Scobie developed a particular affection for Doncaster.

Although he never did win the oldest classic in The Racing Calendar - The St. Leger. Not surprisingly he fell under the spell of the Town Moor Course which had captured the heart of many a racing man before him. Regarded as one of the best and fairest tracks in the country, Doncaster is undoubtedly impressive, with records showing that racing took place there as far back as 1595 with a history of almost four hundred years of horseracing it comes across as a locality steeped in Racing traditions.

The sky hangs like a great dome over the wide course, which, viewed from the Stands, appears to stretch out into a distant horizon and all inanimate growth - trees, grass and the very earth itself, seem pickled in nostalgia. Even the plate glass and chromium of the modern stand erected in 1968, cannot detract from the feeling of the past and the present fused into an element of timelessness. And when the last race has been run and the shadows start to lengthen, do not linger to gaze upon this expanse of green suddenly grown quiet after the tumult of the day. If you would keep your heart whole, go swiftly from this place.

Scobie, as have many of the Racing fraternity based in the South, often stayed in Doncaster for several days at a time. These visits he relished, for true Northern hospitality was always extended to him. Over the years he often stayed at the Danum Hotel, situated in the centre of the town, and soon found himself treated as an honoured guest. Nothing was ever too much trouble for the staff, and when the time came for his departure they would not think of allowing him to leave without a daintily garnished pack of sandwiches, wrapped in a lacy doily, just in case their favourite V.I.P. should be overtaken by hunger pangs on his journey home.

It is not possible to list the many racecourses and their surroundings which gave pleasure to

Scobie - they are too numerous to mention. It is enough to say that British Racing with this infinite variety brought an added pleasure to his Racing days.

It was at Leicester that Scobie rode his last winner of 1963 when making all the running to win by five lengths on Propriano in The Stoughton Plate. This victory brought his total for the season to one hundred and seventy-six, just one ahead of Lester Piggott who finished second in the jockeys' table with one hundred and seventy-five; in third place was Doug Smith with one hundred and twenty one. This victory, won by the shortest possible margin, gave Scobie the championship title for the third year running, and although classic victories had eluded him, he had little to regret. He was champion jockey once again and had completed a hat trick that was truly magical. He embarked on his Winter holiday in high spirits. What he could not know as he left for warmer climes, was that the coming Flat Racing season would see one of his fondest dreams become a reality. The Spring of 1964 might seem a little late for receiving a present from Santa Claus, but from Scobie's point of view, the timing of this event was nothing less than perfect.

# A PRESENT FROM SANTA CLAUS

With four championships to his name, Scobie had every reason to be proud. Twelve years had passed since he talked of retiring and at the age of fifty he had lost nothing ˜f his brilliance in the saddle, if anything he was riding better than before. He had ended the previous season as champion once again with one hundred and seventy-six winners. Yet still he longed for the glittering prize that had now eluded him for thirteen years - The Epsom Derby.

Just before Christmas 1963, the Irish trainer Mick Rogers phoned Scobie to say he had a very good colt entered for The Derby and very much hoped that he would be free to ride him at Epsom. Scobie promised to let him know as soon as he was sure that he had no commitments to his own retainers, and in the Spring, he was able to agree to the engagement to ride Santa Claus in the Epsom classic.

A bay colt by the 1945 St. Leger winner Chamossaire out of Aunt Clara, Santa Claus was not the best looking entry for The Derby. He was a rather plain colt, lean and lanky, straight in the shoulder and possessing allegedly dubious points. But handsome is as handsome does and Mick Rogers impressed with Santa's work on the home gallops, wanted to engage the best jockey he could find to ride him in the 1964 Derby which in this year was worth over seventy-two thousand pounds to the winner - more than double the value of any previous "Blue Riband".

Rogers knew that Scobie was the ideal choice and was delighted when he accepted the mount. But before that could take place, Santa Claus was engaged to run in the Irish Two Thousand Guineas and Scobie was asked to ride him in that race, but unfortunately he was claimed to ride in a moderate maiden race at Newmarket. So on 16th May 1964, with soggy conditions underfoot, he was ridden to victory by the Irish jockey W. Burke. His three lengths win from Young Christopher was received with exuberant enthusiasm. Every Irishman at The Curragh that day felt sure he had seen the winner of the Epsom Derby.

Mick Rogers now felt he should take the colt over to England well in advance of the big day. He was to be flown over, and hidden away in the stables at Kempton Park where, it was hoped, he would be well settled before he had to face his biggest test. But when the colt was taken to the airport, an air strike made it impossible for him to leave for his destination and his trainer had to take him home, only to be informed at four o'clock in the morning, that he should return to the airport right away, which he did, and was soon on a flight to England.

Scobie went over to ride Santa Claus for the first time on the morning before The Derby and found that the colt moved well and felt right.

Derby Day arrived. Scobie did not go to ride work on the morning of the big race. He had his usual breakfast in bed and read the newspapers until it was time to get up and get ready for the races. Then his chauffeur, Bruce, was at the door ready to drive Scobie and his wife to Epsom. It was a nice day and as always on Derby Day there was an almost tangible excitement in the air. Scobie had one ride in an earlier race, but with no success.

The time came to go down to the parade ring and meet the joint owners of Santa Claus, Mr. John Ismay and Mrs. Darby Rogers, mother of Mick Rogers. The colt was calm. In the pre-Derby Parade he remained cool, unlike some of the other competitors who, sensing the excitement of the enormous crowd, began to show signs of restlessness. Horses are quick to pick up any stress or tension around them and it takes a horse of wonderful temperament not to get upset in the atmosphere surrounding The Derby.

Santa Claus moved well as he went down to the start. He had been drawn on the inside, but Scobie felt the draw to be an unimportant factor, for he planned to let his mount take his time in the early stages. All he was concerned about was getting over to the rails by the time they reached the seven-furlong marker; and sure enough by that point in the race Scobie had Santa Claus on the rail, though still a long way back. They came down to Tattenham Corner and into the straight with about six other horses in front of them.

The horse was full of running and did all that Scobie asked of him, as one by one they wore down the opposition. Running into the dip, Scobie saw Jimmy Lindley ahead on Indiana and the thought crossed his mind that the young jockey must be thinking that the race was his for the taking. But Scobie knew that he had Indiana well covered and headed his rival inside the final eighty yards, to win by a length.

So at last the dream came true. After thirteen attempts Scobie had at last won The Derby at the age of fifty. Riding back with a police escort to the unsaddling enclosure, it all seemed unreal. He could see his wife May standing at the entrance gate smiling at him, tears of joy in her eyes. The young Irish jockey, Burke, who had ridden Santa to victory in the Irish Two Thousand Guineas was also there, very excited and full of congratulations. And there was more excitement still to come when, after weighing in, Scobie was invited up to the Royal Box where The Queen, Prince Philip and The Queen Mother told him how delighted they were, as they knew he had been trying to win The Derby for so long. Soon he was surrounded by Press reporters, some asking the almost inevitable question "Will you retire now that you have won The

Derby?" to which Scobie was quick to reply "No, Sir Gordon wouldn't like that - and I want to do it again anyway." That evening Scobie and his wife gave a party, and even then it all seemed unreal to this great jockey who, hours after the race had been won, was saying "I won't really believe it until I read the result in tomorrow's papers."

Scobie was on "cloud nine". It seemed that everything was going his way. For years he had dreamed of riding The Derby winner, and now, at last, the dream had become a reality. Nor was this his only reason to feel proud and happy, for if winning The Derby were not enough excitement for one week, daughter Loretta had made him a grandfather for the second time, only a few days before his Epsom triumph. For all the Breasley family 1964 was truly a year to remember.

Now that a Derby victory was his, Scobie longed to repeat his performance, though in the following season, in The Derby, won by Sea Bird, he could only take sixth place on Cambridge. However in 1966 it was to be a very different story.

Charlottown was impeccably bred, being by Charlottsville out of that great race-mare Meld. Owned by Lady Zia Werner and trained by Gordon Smyth, he was due to make his first appearance of the season in the Brighton Derby Trial on 9th May. The big crowd at the seaside course were hoping to see how he would perform, but in fact he was found to be suffering from a bruised foot that morning and was unable to run. Only sixteen days to go before The Derby. Charlottown's injury caused him to drift in the anti-post market to 20-1. However, he was fit to compete in the Lingfield Derby Trial on 13th May.

Ron Hutchinson, fellow Australian and great friend of Scobie, was riding Charlottown for the first time. He wanted to give his mount as un-exacting a race as possible but he allowed the colt to take things too easily in the early stages of the

72

race and by half-way was at the tail-end of the field.   Black Prince II entered the straight at least twenty lengths. ahead of Charlottown; two furlongs out Charlottown made extremely rapid progress, but then he began to hang badly to the left.   Hutchinson had to stop riding in order to straighten him up.   From then on he had no chance of catching Black Prince II, who beat him by three lengths and poor Ron Hutchinson came in for some fearful criticism.   It therefore came as no surprise when it was announced that Scobie would partner Charlottown at Epsom.   At first he had felt some reluctance about accepting the mount.   Ron Hutchinson was a close friend and Scobie was not happy with the idea of taking a good Derby prospect away from him.   Yet he knew that if he refused the ride, it would be given to another jockey in any case, and with no chance of Ron being engaged to ride Charlottown, Scobie accepted.

Ron Hutchinson was a light-weight jockey, and one of the best in the game.   But Charlottown was not the most compliant animal ever to set hoof on a racecourse and probably needed a bigger, stronger rider to give his best.

Once he had accepted the mount, Scobie began to feel an excited anticipation.   Perhaps that second Derby victory was just around the corner.   Then, with only two days to go to Derby Day, Scobie took a crashing fall at Windsor.   It looked as though Charlottown would have to be ridden by another jockey after all.   But Scobie was tough, determined, and not a man whose nerve was easily shaken.   He declared himself fit to ride at Epsom and proved it when he rode two winners on the opening day of the meeting.

Came Derby Day.   Scobie was in the parade ring with the owner and trainer.   Charlottown was led over by his lad and Scobie was about to mount him when the colt trod on his own off fore and spread a plate.   A nerve-racking delay followed while Gordon Smyth's own blacksmith, George Windless, re-plated Charlottown, a very tricky business since the colt suffered from thin-soled feet and the slightest mistake on the blacksmith's part could have resulted in withdrawal from the race. Millions of television viewers shared the suspense as the new plate was nailed in place. The colt took a few strides, there was no limp. Scobie was quickly into the saddle and away went Charlottown to join the others down at the start.

In the early stages of the race, Right Noble and St. Puckle went into the lead. After half a mile Charlottown was well to the rear of the field, with only three horses behind him. Scobie could seldom be lured away from the rails, but this time he had to come away from the rails in order to pass St. Puckle and Right Noble. He was asked to make his run in the final furlong, but then found the way blocked by Black Prince II and Pretendre. Scobie had to switch Charlottown back to the rails even though this meant losing ground. Just inside the final furlong Pretendre led Charlottown by a neck. However, Scobie, cool as ever, brought his mount up on the inside to win by a neck. This was undoubtedly one of the greatest rides in his career. Never was his capacity for rapid thinking better demonstrated.

Scobie was a happy and contented man on Derby Day 1966. He had now ridden two Derby winners and been champion jockey four times. He felt that he had every reason to be proud and now looked forward to partnering Charlottown in his future races. But sadly this was not to be. When the horse made his next appearance on the race-course, Scobie was side-lined through injury and Jimmy Lindley was engaged to ride in his place. Scobie saw nothing wrong with that arrangement, but fully expected to ride Charlottown again once he recovered from his injuries. But the horse's owner had arranged for Lindley to ride him in all his future races, perhaps thinking this to be a fair return for his stepping in to fill the gap when Scobie was unavailable. Scobie, however, felt mistreated by this decision. After all, he had ridden Charlottown to victory in The Derby, no less a victory for the owner than for himself and he felt, as did many others, that he had been treated discourteously. Yet for all that, Scobie was resilient enough to take such set-backs and misunderstandings in his stride. He was happy with his two Derby wins and although he would dearly have loved to ride a Derby winner for Sir Gordon, this was not to be. He did not have an addition to the family to celebrate after his second Derby win. Although he did not know it then, it was to be five years later, three years after retiring from the saddle, that much to his delight, Loretta would present him with his first grandson, a little boy called Jason.

In April 1967, fellow Australian George Moore arrived in England to replace Lester Piggott, by then turned free-lance, as first jockey to Noel Murless at Warren Place.

It looked like being an exciting and successful season for the new partnership, which by September would have brought the stable winnings to a quarter of a million pounds, but long before this impressive figure was reached, they had landed The Two Thousand Guineas - One Thousand Guineas double, the colts classic being won by Royal Palace, a son of Scobie's old favourite, the great Ballymoss. As a two-year-old, Royal Palace had won The Acomb Stakes at York and the one mile Royal Lodge Stakes at Ascot. In the latter race he lost half a dozen lengths at the start and was the back marker on the final bend; many rated this a brilliant performance.

The winner of the fillies classic was Fleet, a magnificent bay, who, in spite of having won The Cheveley Park Stakes the previous Autumn, had disgraced herself in her preliminary outing of 1967 by refusing to line up for the Classic Trial at New-market; she went to the front in The One Thousand Guineas when still over a furlong from home and kept going to beat 66-1 chance St. Pauli Girl by half a length, with Lacquer a head away third.

In winning The Two Thousand Guineas, Royal Palace had emulated Crepello, who ten years previously had won the race on his first appearance of the season.

In The Derby, Royal Palace started favourite at 7-4. Fifth at Tattenham Corner, he moved smoothly, but Piggott's mount Ribocco was not going down without a struggle, and at one point, after Royal Palace had gone into the lead, he almost drew level with the favourite; but the leader had a little in reserve and when Moore gave him a couple of taps with the whip, he accelerated to win by two and a half lengths, with Scobie's mount Dart Board finishing strongly to take third place.

With three classic victories achieved in the first three months of the season, the new partnership at Warren Place seemed all set for a bright future; and in July that year George Moore had the added pleasure of seeing his son Gary make his debut as a jockey at Le Tremblay at the tender age of fifteen years.

Behind the scenes, however, all was not well for this man who looked to have a great chance of bringing home a Triple Crown winner - the first since Bahram in 1935. Unknown to the racing public, disturbing elements were at work to destroy Moore's peace of mind.

However, the chances of victory in The St. Leger for Royal Palace still appeared promising, and the colt missed several tempting engagements to concentrate on his preparation for this final classic of the season. It had been intended to run him in that recognised trial for The St. Leger; The Great Voltiger Stakes, but unfortunately he rapped himself on the gallops and did not run. His injury was thought to be of a trivial nature when he worked well on September 2nd and the Press carried headlines stating that he was certain to run in The Leger, but on September 9th, only three days before the big race was due to be run, his trainer Noel Murless was very concerned by the fact that the colt blew hard after work; and after a conference with owner Jim Joel, Royal Palace was taken out of The St. Leger.

George Moore was bitterly disappointed, but he had other problems on his mind when he made a weekend visit to France to see his son Gary ride. On returning to his flat in London's Gadogan Square, accompanied by his wife, son John and daughter Michelle; the family found all their clothes, even those of ten-year-old Michelle, slashed into pieces and ruined.

Soon the national Press told a horrifying story, and for the first time the public became aware of the threats made to Moore over the preceding three months when he stated "These gangsters follow me around all the time. They are vicious, spiteful and apparently will stop at nothing. They have made my life hell for several months." A fearful story unfolded. Phone calls from an unknown source had threatened dire consequences if the jockey refused to obey instructions to pull certain horses. For months the Moores had been frightened to let their young daughter out of sight. The Racing world was shocked, and trainer Peter Cazalet said, "This virtually amounts to someone trying to chase Moore out of the country." In spite of all this George Moore vehemently denied rumours that he would not ride as first jockey to Murless in 1968; yet in the end, with the safety of his family uppermost in his mind, he felt compelled to return to ride in Australia; although he did continue riding in England until the end of the 1967 Flat Racing season.

The British public did not have time to know him well, but it is interesting to note that even during that stressful period of his life, George Moore was not impervious to the needs of others; for in October of that troubled year, he came to hear of the distress of stable lad Tony Moss, who on learning that the racehorse in his care - Vibrant - was to be sold to an Australian stud farm, decided that he must emigrate also, saying "where Vibrant goes, I must go." George, touched by such loyalty, promptly offered the lad a house in Australia, and Tony, his wife and four-year-old daughter, set sail for their new home on the same ship as the horse.

1968 saw George Moore back riding on the Australian turf. But his troubles were not over, and in April of that year he received letters demanding huge sums of money and warnings that his life would be in danger if he refused to pay. A tape recording was put through his letter box; on playing it he heard a voice saying that he and his wife would soon have their necks broken.

Around the same time blackmail letters were received by three racehorse owners; Lloyd Foyster and Rod Miller were each asked to pay fifteen thousand pounds protection money against a murder syndicate. Owner Stan Fox was asked for ten thousand pounds. The letters varied in content. The extortionist obviously made a study of each of his victims - whether they had families and the nature of their property - and made his threats to fit the situation.

George Moore continued his career as a jockey; he refused to be intimidated and eventually retired from the saddle in 1970. He received the O.B.E. in 1972. At the time of his retirement he said, "You've got to be young and strong to be a jockey," which evoked the comment that fellow countryman Scobie Breasley, whilst undoubtedly strong, could by no stretch of the imagination be described as young. To this George replied "Oh well, as for him - he's just a blinking marvel!"

# SCOBIE AND THE PRESS

Scobie's activities on and off the racecourse were followed closely by the Press. Mostly their accounts were accurate and informative. But unfortunately there were times when Scobie must have wished that Racing journalists would become an extinct breed, for on certain occasions they treated him none too gently.

Perhaps the worst kind of reporting to come Scobie's way was a style of writing which, while appearing to be quite innocuous on the surface, was anything but when a little reading between the lines was applied. Indeed not every writer even took the trouble to keep their inept scribblings decently between any lines, but openly wrote any amount of unmitigated nonsense in the name of journalism. Some of the worst examples of this kind of writing appeared the day after Scobie won his first Derby on Santa Claus. One writer went so far as to say that "Old Scobie Breasley, the grandaddy of the turf, only needs a long white beard to look like a real-life Santa Claus."

This sort of thing may have been very amusing to some people, and if the journalist responsible had confined himself to just one sentence written in rather poor taste, his article might not have warranted anything but the mildest criticism. But, alas, he did not confine himself to a few rather ill chosen words, but continued in similar vein going on to describe May Breasley as being dressed up in a pink Mayfair-tailored suit and looking down with a childlike awe at what he had the impertinence to call "her diminutive husband". As the writer of this article was a professional journalist, one might suppose he would understand that to say a lady was dressed in a pink suit would be a perfectly acceptable description. But to say that she was *dressed up* in a pink suit gives the sentence a very different connotation. And it is reasonable to suppose that Scobie's wife, barely an inch taller than he, would have experienced considerable difficulty should she have wished to look down on him with childlike awe, or any other expression.

Towards the end of Scobie's career as a jockey, a certain section of the Press appear to have been obsessed with his age. Of course, his riding ability was remarkable for his age, a fact on which a constant and rather tedious emphasis was laid. The point which many writers failed to get across, was the fact that his achievements in the saddle would have been remarkable at any age. Luckily Scobie remained philosophical. He knew that fame has its price and it seemed that part of the price meant enduring a certain amount of journalism which, although in no way libellous, was frequently lacking in good taste.

On one occasion, Scobie, normally patient and considerate to reporters, feeling that the subject of his age was becoming somewhat over-worked, was rather evasive when questioned yet again on this subject. Next day the reporter took his revenge by writing "When it comes to discussing his age, Scobie Breasley reminds one of an ageing actress".

And once when reporting Scobie's defeat on a highly fancied runner, the same writer, speculating on the reason for this defeat, suggested that the cold weather had perhaps got into those old bones, thus affecting the jockey's riding abilities. This time he had gone too far and Scobie, seeking him out at the next race meeting, dealt with him in a manner that was far from gentle. It was generally felt that such treatment was richly deserved.

In 1961 two Racing journalists wrote articles whose implications were such that Scobie felt he could not take the law into his own hands this time. He sought legal advice and as a result of this felt obliged to bring libel actions against Odhams Press, proprietors, printers and publishers of

The Sporting Life, and The Daily Herald and against Mr. Tom Nickalls and Mr. Don Cox of Long Acre, W.C.2., the writers of the articles published in these newspapers.

On 12th November 1963 in the High Court of Justice, Queen's Bench Division, before Mr. Justice Havers, the consolidated libel actions were begun.

In The Daily Herald of 9th November 1961, Mr. Cox wrote an article headed "Breasley is barracked after losing the last" and reading: "A small group of punters stood at the entrance of the unsaddling enclosure and bellowed insults at Scobie Breasley because he failed to win the last race yesterday. They accused Breasley of not trying after he was beaten on the odds-on favourite Indian Conquest and implied he had lost the race to benefit the bookmakers.

"Go back to Australia" they shouted in Scobie's face as he brought Indian Conquest through their middle and into the unsaddling enclosure.

"Is this another for the bookmakers?" they jeered. "Another for Swift". The name of this London West End bookmaker was mentioned because his son Brian is married to Scobie Breasley's daughter - Loretta. Breasley, although flushed in the face by the volume of barracking with which the disgruntled punters greeted him, did not answer their insults while he unsaddled Indian Conquest, but the demonstration was too much for trainer Ken Cundell. Ken had no runner in the four-horse Arlington Stakes. He was a by-stander on this occasion and took the barrackers to task. Seizing the arm of the loudest voiced critic, Cundell demanded that they all looked closely at both horses standing in the winner's enclosure where the winner Utrillo II looked unruffled by his efforts to win the mile race while the loser sweated a great deal. Faced with such an authoritative opinion, the demonstration fizzled out and it was freely admitted they were speaking through their pockets.

Best Form. Of the four runners in the Arlington Stakes, Indian Conquest did hold the best overall form, but it must be remembered that this three-year-old had had a hard race in The Cambridgeshire while the ex-Italian trained horse, Utrillo II, had won his previous race in modest company. What annoyed the barrackers yesterday was the position - last of the four - that Breasley had chosen for Indian Conquest before he started his challenge two furlongs from the winning post. The loud mouthed gents yesterday overlooked the similar style which Breasley has adopted on the Brighton course - over which he is the undisputed champion rider. On this and other courses he has shown himself a master of tactics and I accept his judgment. Breasley won a race earlier in the day, the Highclere Nursery on Remainder after a low draw (position four) had lessened his chance. Scobie won against the draw at the previous Newbury meeting and he felt convinced he could do so again. This winner brings his season's total to one hundred and sixty-seven."

Mr. Breasley claimed that the article injured him in his character and reputation.

The defendants denied that the words bore or were capable of bearing any meaning defamatory of Mr. Breasley or that he suffered any injury.

They also contended that the article was written in good faith and without malice; was a true report of events which had taken place and was published for the information of the public.

Mr. Gerald Gardiner, Q.C. and Mr. L.J. Belcourt appeared for Mr. Breasley. Mr. J.T. Molony, Q.C. and Mr. Hugh Davidson for the defendants.

Mr. Gardiner said that Mr. Breasley was an Australian jockey and began riding when he was fourteen years of age. Last week he became Champion Jockey, winning the championship by a short head. The most important quality in a jockey was not his hands nor his great experience, but his reputation for integrity. That was simple enough, for sometimes odds-on favourites lost, to the benefit of bookmakers. It was possible for a jockey to pull a horse, to restrain it deliberately from winning and if a group of bookmakers could be sure that an odds-on favourite would not win, a great deal of money could be made. Until the matters complained of, Mr. Breasley had always borne the highest reputation as a jockey. Owners and trainers would not risk employing any jockey reasonably suspected of pulling a horse.

Referring to Mr. Nickalls' article Counsel said that the only reasons why a rider did not shine on odds-on horses were either that he was incompetent or was pulling the horse. Both allegations were untrue in the case of Mr. Breasley. No one could suggest that he was incompetent; up to the time he had ridden fifty-five odds-on mounts, he had won on thirty-six and lost on nineteen. Mr. Nickalls must have known that there was no foundation in the allegation. The article caused a great deal of discussion among jockeys, trainers and owners. Some of whom would give evidence.

Scobie said "I don't know if these men set out to do me any harm, but they could have done me a lot of harm." And to his knowledge no one had ever before suggested that he had been paid by bookmakers to pull horses.

The trainer, Mr. Stafford Ingham said in giving evidence that it was everything for an owner and trainer to know that they could rely on their jockey. He had known Scobie for about ten years and had he not known him so well, on reading the article he might well have thought "something fishy" was going on after reading it.

Sir Gordon Richards gave evidence. He said that he had been a jockey for thirty-five years and had ridden against Mr. Breasley, who was hard to beat in any race. Since becoming a trainer he had retained Mr. Breasley because he regarded him as a brilliant jockey and a man of integrity. A jockey who never tried to win when riding an odds-on favourite would not be a jockey for long.

The hearing was adjourned to be resumed next day.

Mr. Nickalls was questioned about his phrase that Mr. Breasley "never seems to shine on odds-on horses". Mr. Nickalls said he meant to say that luck did not seem to run for him on odds-on chances in the same way as it did not run for him in classic races.

Mr. Justice Havers said "But there was no mention of classics in the article."

Mr. Cox, giving evidence, said that he did not doubt Mr. Breasley's integrity and considered him to be a master tactician and the article did not convey to him that Mr. Breasley had tried to lose. Cross-examined by Mr. Gardiner, the witness agreed that no more serious allegation could be made against a jockey than that he tried to pull a horse for a bookmaker.

The hearing was adjourned until next day - 14th November 1963.

His Lordship, on the verdicts of the jury, entered judgment for Mr. Breasley for two hundred and fifty pounds damage in respect of publication in The Daily Herald and judgment for the defendants, with costs, in respect of publication in The Sporting Life.

His Lordship ordered payment out of the defendants of the balance of the five hundred pounds which had been paid into Court.

The jury had retired at three-twenty-five p.m. and returned at five-fifteen p.m. finding for the plaintiff in respect of The Daily Herald article and for the defendants in respect of the article in The Sporting Life, assessing damages at two hundred and fifty pounds.

Scobie, therefore, was awarded two hundred

and fifty pounds. But the costs he would have to pay would amount to ten times the damages. The total cost of the three day action amounted to about five thousand pounds. Scobie's claim for damages for The Sporting Life article was dismissed. Altogether it seems to have been a very expensive way of clearing the name of a man whose integrity should not have been called into question.

While most famous men learn to expect a certain amount of adverse publicity, it would appear that Scobie received more than his fair share of this type of journalism. Fortunately such writers were in a minority; the greater part wrote with fairness and accuracy. Some journalists became personal friends, notably the charming, erudite racing correspondent of the Daily Express, Peter O'Sullevan. And in 1968 The Sunday Express published "Scobie the Maestro", a short biography by Tom Forrest whose accuracy could not be faulted.

# A MAN'S MAN

Scobie's love of sport extended far beyond racing and included tennis, golf, water-skiing and swimming. He was also a keen spectator and thought tennis the most wonderful game to watch. He liked to get to Wimbledon whenever possible, but this was a rare treat for Scobie on account of his riding commitments. Yet he was determined to follow the matches as closely as possible and during Wimbledon week never went to the races without his portable radio set so that he could listen to the commentaries between riding in races.

Scobie's interest in professional tennis began in his teenage years and he remembered watching Jack Crawford, the Australian winner of the Wimbledon Men's Singles Championship of 1933. But the greatest game he ever watched was the Wimbledon Semi-final between fellow Australian Ken Rosewall and the American Vic Seixas in 1956. Rosewall was down 1-2 after three sets, then he levelled; was 2-5 down in the final set, but was able to beat his opponent in a sensational match in which Seixas constantly complained about line decisions and boos. "I was more tired than Rosewall at the end" laughed Scobie. In the final later that week Rosewall was beaten by the player who Scobie rated the greatest ever on his day - Lew Hoad. And when Neil Fraser, a close friend who lived in Melbourne at the same time as Scobie, beat Rod Laver in the Wimbledon Championhsip of 1960, Scobie felt as though he had played every shot himself.

When questioned about the proficiency of his own game, Scobie would always claim that he was no better than average, but on the evidence of those who saw him play, this must be taken as a typically modest assessment and but for cartilage trouble earlier in his life, it is possible that he could have reached championship level.

His other great love - golf - took up much of his precious spare time. Scobie would have been happy to play every day if given the chance, but his busy life did not allow for this. Naturally, many of his closest friendships were with men who shared his passion for the golf course, notably fellow jockeys Ron Hutchinson and Geoff Lewis.

At the time Scobie came to ride in England, Geoff was still a teenager, but young though he was he already possessed potential which the senior jockey was quick to recognise. In no time at all Geoff Lewis became Scobie's protege. The boy tried to model himself on Scobie and though their riding style differed they often thought alike. Also a keen golfer, Geoff was to spend many hours partnering Scobie on the links. This was not all sweetness and light by any means, for Scobie could lose patience if his game did not go according to plan and Lewis relates the amusing tale of the time when Scobie, missing a putt at Leatherhead, became so incensed that he threw his putter into the air. Unfortunately it landed high in a birch tree and was only dislodged after they had spent twenty minutes throwing bricks at it.

Another occasion Geoff Lewis recalls with amusement is the time when he, Scobie and several other British jockeys, including Bill Rickaby, Jimmy Lindley, Joe Sime, Joe Mercer and Harry Carr, were invited to ride in Sweden during The World Fair in Stockholm. They had an uncomfortable flight in a small plane which, before landing at Copenhagen, ran into a severe storm. This storm, apart from prolonging the journey, also served to ruin the enjoyment of the gourmet picnic hamper provided by Bill Rickaby. It was well into the early hours of the morning before Scobie and Geoff settled down to sleep, as Scobie, always fond of his food, had insisted on going out in search of a meal despite their late arrival.

Geoff Lewis, recalling the scene, says "It

seemed that no sooner had we got off to sleep
than there was a knock at the door - it was the
boys saying it was time to go to catch the plane
for Stockholm.   But Scobie was still half asleep,
with less than an hour to get to the airport.   While
he was washing and shaving, I tried to speed things
up by laying out his clothes, vest, pants, shirt, tie,
socks and a grey suit.   He came out of the bathroom still at a leisurely pace and said 'I want to
wear my blue suit.'   I rushed to the case, pulled
out the blue suit, back goes the grey suit.   We get
to the airport and the boys have held up the plane.
Once on board, Scobie says to me 'See what
happens when you keep me out half the night.'   I
said 'Me! keeping you out, I like that.'   Anyway he
said that as soon as we landed in Sweden he would
be off to the hotel to catch a couple of hours
sleep before going racing.

"However, as we were being driven in a mini-
bus from the airport, we saw a signpost pointing in
the direction of Stockholm, but the bus was taking
a different route.   Scobie spotted this and asked
the driver why we were not taking the road to
Stockholm.   The driver replied 'Oh, we think we
take you to race course, you look at race course,
we give you breakfast.'   Scobie, anxious to get
some rest said 'Breakfast!   I don't want any bloody
breakfast, I just want to sleep for a while.'   'Sorry,
Mr. Breasley' said the driver and continued in the
direction of the course.   We arrived at ten o'clock
and the first race was not until two-thirty.   We
felt pretty fed up, but after a beer and a sauna
even Scobie felt a bit better; they gave us lunch
and we went down to ride in the first race.   Unfortunately for us it had been raining cats and dogs
and as the track was not grass but sand, Scobie
came back after the first race covered in dirty wet
sand and looking like Al Jolson.   'That's enough for
me' he said, 'I think I'll only ride in the two big
races.'   He was booked for five rides.   So when the

Chairman came down Scobie put it very nicely to him 'Look' he said 'I have had a long journey over here, I think I'd best only ride in the two big races,' so this official said 'Well, Mr. Breasley, it will be a very big trouble getting you off the other two horses' and Scobie replied 'It'll be bloody bigger trouble trying to get me on them I can tell you!' " And as far as he was concerned, that was the end of the argument. Geoff had to get the colours, and ride the horses concerned; getting beaten on one, but winning on the other.

Although he was not given to over-indulgence, it could never be said that Scobie could not hold his liquor. Yet the lavish hospitality extended to the British jockeys by their Swedish hosts proved to be too much even for him, and after a dinner, given in their honour at which the champagne flowed freely, the evening ended with Scobie doing "Knees up Mother Brown" in a fountain, dressed in his best suit and wearing good brogue shoes which were always carefully polished and kept on trees.

He returned to England with a terrible hang-over, four pounds over-weight and with six rides at Alexander Park the same day. It was undoubtedly not one of Scobie's better days; he felt like a wreck. As Geoff Lewis put it "He looked bad, and when he looks bad, he really looks bad!"

At one point in the afternoon all the jockeys were down at the start except Scobie who was only just coming out of the weighing room. A steward said "Come on Breasley, hurry up or we will fine you."

"Do what you like" replied Scobie, "The way I feel you can disqualify me for life for all I care!" So much for Swedish racing!

Listening to Geoff Lewis talking about the man who was his mentor in his early days, and later his close friend, one cannot fail to notice the warmth that Scobie inspired in his friends. Speak to any one of them and they will leave you with the impression that here was a man who could twist them around his little finger; exasperating and endearing, he would infuriate them one minute and have them helpless with laughter the next.

Fellow jockey, Harry Carr, who retired from riding to take on a farm near Newmarket, remembers the time when Scobie, always fond of dogs, decided to buy a labrador puppy as a present for his grand-children. Unfortunately soon after arriving at his new home in Epsom, Tippytail chewed up the new riding boots of Scobie's son-in-law, Brian Swift, which caused Scobie to feel that the puppy might be a more suitable present for Harry Carr rather than for Zonda and Kelly. Tippytail was duly handed over and trained to be a gun dog at the Newmarket farm.

The Breasley's had always been a dog-loving family and during their early days in England, whilst living in flats, they much regretted being unable to keep a dog. This was soon to be put to rights when they moved to Heather Brae, their house in Putney, for it was not long before Bing, an alsation, appeared on the scene. Scobie named the dog in honour of the singer Bing Crosby and one suspects this was as much a tribute to Bing's prowess as a golfer as to the quality of his voice. When Scobie had to face the moment which every dog lover dreads - the death of his dog - he very sensibly brought home another alsation puppy who became Bing II. If Scobie had paid a compliment to the great American singer, he was himself paid a similar compliment years later when his god-son, Garry Lewis, son of jockey Geoff Lewis, telephoned to ask if Scobie had any objection to having a bull terrier puppy named after him. When the animal had arrived at the Lewis's home, the boy could not decide on a suitable name, then his father said "You know, that dog looks just like Uncle Scobie." After that there could be no other name for him.

Scobie's firm friendship with jockey Ron

Hutchinson also developed from a boyhood admiration on the latter's part. Like Geoff Lewis, Ron admired Scobie's horsemanship from an early age. In fact he had had the opportunity to see his idol in action from his earliest days in racing, for he was a fellow countryman, and by the time Ron was an apprentice in Australia Scobie was already a mature jockey at the top of his profession.

Ten years after Scobie came to ride in England, "Hutchie", as he was known to his friends and colleagues, left Australia for Ireland where he was to ride as first jockey to Paddy Prendergast, the Irish trainer, who, in his youth, had ridden in England under National Hunt Rules, and in due course became top trainer in England three years running. Hutchie's association with the Prendergast stable soon gave him his first victory in an English classic, when the chestnut colt, Martial, won the 1960 Two Thousand Guineas. As a first win in England it was a most auspicious beginning for this young man who, later, was to become first jockey to John Dunlop's Arundel stable which housed the large string of racehorses owned by the Duke of Norfolk. This proved a most successful appointment for all concerned, and Ron Hutchinson was soon to be rated one of the best light-weight riders in the game; gregarious and good natured he made the perfect foil to Scobie's deceptively dour, taciturn appearance. Hutchie and Scobe - a great team on and off the racecourse.

The golf course often saw them together and when staying away from home for racing they usually dined together. One such occasion is laughingly remembered by Hutchie, who recalls the time during Leger Week at Doncaster when he and Scobie arranged a get-together after racing. When he first arrived in Ireland he had stayed for some time with his good friends - Moira and Joe McLaughlin. Now the couple were over here for the Leger Meeting and had been invited to join

91

Scobie and a few friends at dinner. The party met in the bar at the Danum Hotel, where Scobie was staying, and after having a drink and choosing their meal from the menu, they were called to their table. The surroundings were pleasant, the company congenial and the food delicious. However, after eating the second course, Scobie said he thought the grouse had been rather on the small side and suggested to his companions that they might like to join him in yet another helping. Everyone declined the offer except Mr. McLaughlin who, together with his host, partook of yet another portion of grouse complete with the accompanying vegetables and trimmings, while their amused friends sat waiting to join them when the dessert was served.

Scobie's friendships tended to endure, often bonded together by mutual sporting interests. Yet his love of golf could sometimes cause him to be unmindful of other arrangements, as on the occasion when he agreed to be the "castaway" in the popular B.B.C. programme "Desert Island Discs". Roy Plomley relates the story of a slight misdemeanor. "I arranged with Scobie that we would make an afternoon recording, but at nine o'clock on the morning of the appointed day, a member of his household staff telephoned to say that Mr. Breasley had been called urgently to Newmarket for some trials and would it be possible please to postpone the recording until another day? Obviously I agreed. During the afternoon I telephoned his house to see if he had returned so that we could fix another date. I found myself speaking to another member of the household staff - 'Mr. Breasley is not back from the golf course yet Sir' she said - it was a fine day and I did not blame him a bit."

Scobie had a reputation as a singer and at jockeys' dinners and similar functions he often obliged with a song. Very often it was the old favourite of his "It had to be you". This was one of his choices in "Desert Island Discs" when he at last managed to tear himself away from the golf course long enough to make the recording. He chose the version by Count Basie and his orchestra. He also wanted to hear Raymond Glendenning giving a Derby commentary, but it was not on a race that Scobie himself was in. The selection of records may have left something to be desired from a purely musical standpoint, yet they were entertaining and a reflection of Scobie's preference for music of the lighter kind. He did not find time to study musical appreciation in depth, but he enjoyed music and knew more about it than many racing people, some of whom might easily confuse a tenor and a treble, with a fiver and an each way double.

Scobie enjoyed the good things. He believed in enjoying life and it was fortunate that he did not have the weight problems which many jockeys have to contend with. As it was, he was able to indulge in his love of good food and wine without having to worry too much about dire consequences.

He was also fond of good clothes, always immaculate, his suits carefully pressed, his shoes shining, he was in fact something of a dandy. Nothing annoyed him more than an unkempt appearance. He was never guilty of this himself and it was quite usual for him to bath and change three times a day. He admired smartness in others too and was quick to compliment anyone whose appearance he found pleasing.

His love of cleanliness sometimes evoked the disapproval of his friends, for he was not above cleaning the cutlery on his napkin when dining in their homes. However, they could console themselves with the knowledge that he would do just the same thing when dining in a five star hotel! A very high standard was always maintained in his own home and he saw no reason to settle for less elsewhere.

B.B.C. commentator and ex-jockey, Jimmy

Lindley, remembers Scobie as a "bon viveur". Often a guest at the Breasley home, he found Scobie a delightful host who kept an excellent table and was quite without equal when providing his friends with a Chinese meal. On one such occasion Jimmy and his wife, along with other friends, enjoyed an eight course Chinese meal prepared by Scobie's excellent staff who had come from Hong Kong to look after the domestic arrangements at "Heather Brae". All the guests agreed that it was the best Chinese meal they had ever tasted, and that included meals in Hong Kong and in China itself.

The Lindleys also enjoyed Scobie's hospitality in Barbados where he had another home, used most years as his Winter retreat during the closed season of British Flat Racing. This beach house allowed Scobie, his wife and friends to indulge to the full their love of water ski-ing and swimming. Jimmy remembers walking along the beach with fellow jockey and close friend, Joe Mercer, looking for Scobie's house and meeting their host stripped to the waist, displaying a very hairy chest and aiming for a mahogany tan.

It was usual at Scobie's beach parties for each of the guests to bring along a gallon or so of their own brew of punch. The stone jars were placed in the kitchen, the contents to be consumed later.

Trainer John Sutcliffe, a guest for the first time at one of Scobie's barbecues, went to the kitchen and seeing a jar of liquid asked what it was. Scobie said it was rum punch and offered a glass. John drank it down, pronounced it very good and helped himself to a second which went down well with a few ice cubes. Jimmy Lindley and Joe Mercer joined him, but when he drank a third glassful which went down rather quickly, he suddenly went wild, stripped off his clothes and jumped up on to a large garden table where he proceeded to entertain the assembled company with a dance. Scobie, who had craftily omitted to tell anyone that the punch had not been diluted, was in tears of laughter, but naturally May Breasley was somewhat less amused.

Joe Mercer first met Scobie when, a brilliant apprentice, he often rode against the man from Wagga Wagga. He was, in fact, leading apprentice two years running and also won The Oaks on Lord Astor's Big Game filly Ambiguity in 1953. Joe was present at the jockeys' dinner at the end of the 1951 Flat season when the jockeys had clubbed together to give Scobie a beautiful silver salver as a farewell gift when the Australian rider was returning to his homeland and, as they thought at the time, retiring from his life as a jockey. Little did they know that two years later he would be back among them with the greatest moments of his career still to come.

Joe watched Scobie settle to the English way of racing and living. He admired the impeccable style and quality of his riding. As the younger jockey said "He never left the paint and sometimes it seemed that he must have ducked under the rail and come out further on down the track."

When Scobie suffered the worst accident of his career, the fall from Sayonara at Alexandra Park, his One Thousand Guineas winner Festoon was left without her jockey for The Oaks. The ride went to the young Joe Mercer and although he did not bring her home to victory in the second fillies classic of the season, he brought the lovely chestnut back to the winner's enclosure in The Coronation Cup at Ascot while Scobie was still bravely fighting to overcome the after-effects of that terrible fall.

As the years went by Scobie and Joe strengthened their friendship and respect for one another. Both were to become champion jockeys and each admired the horsemanship of the other.

Joe rates Scobie one of the finest ambassadors Australia could have wished for, along with Scobie's close friends and fellow Australians Bill Williamson

95

and Ron Hutchinson. He calls them "All topping fellows" though when acknowledging the similarity of style between Bill Williamson and Scobie, he laughingly recalls that "Bill had bigger, sharper elbows than Scobie, they did rather get in the way."

One lesson which both Jimmy Lindley and Joe Mercer learned from their earliest days in racing, was never to try to ride a waiting race on Scobie, he could always catch them on the line. Both men speak of him with admiration and, as with all his friends, the warm regard in which they hold him comes through time and time again.

Scobie was also an example and inspiration to many a young rider. Colin Williams, the apprentice who rode Be Friendly to victory in the 1966 Vernons Sprint Cup, just one year before Scobie would achieve the same distinction, thought him to be one of the finest riders and most formidable opponents he had ever encountered. Now, years later, as a trainer at Pangbourne, Berkshire, Colin has never found any reason to revise that opinion. Looking back to the days when riding against the great Australian was a regular occurence, he is full of reminiscences. Above all, he remembers Scobie as a true sportsman, adding weight to this point by recalling a race, run in the days before patrol cameras recorded a jockey's every move, where Scobie came in for some very rough treatment; at one point being very lucky not to be put over the rails. Unsaddling after the race, Colin, indicating the white paint from the rails still visible on one of Scobie's boots, said "A bit rough out there wasn't it?" And the rider who would have been perfectly justified in reporting the unfortunate incident to the stewards, only gave a slight smile and said "Yes, I guess I was a bit unlucky."

Modern technology has virtually eliminated deliberate rough riding and brought the public into closer contact with the complexities of race-riding;

although misunderstandings still arise, these are largely to be found among a certain element who read a race only through the state of their pockets; as in the Guinness Stakes run at Brighton on the 18th May 1966. Red Tears, ridden by Russ Maddock was first past the post, beating Bill Williamson on Make Haste by half a length, with odds-on favourite Tadolina, ridden by Scobie, running into third; each of the three horses involved in the finish being ridden by Australian jockeys. However, after holding an enquiry, the stewards disqualified Red Tears and awarded the race, not to the second horse Make Haste, but to Scobie's mount Tadolina.

This decision caused much disquiet among the backers of the relegated horses; Red Tears being returned at 13-2, at one point having touched 7-1; while Make Haste, after opening at 8-1 had drifted in the market to 10's. Angry comments were to be heard on the terraces, the least savage being along the lines of - "That bloody Breasley gets away with blue murder!"

Poor Scobie, he came in for some black looks when next he emerged from the weighing room. His critics did not appear to realise that the enquiry had been instigated solely by the stewards, and not as a result of Scobie objecting to the winner.

If, on this occasion he won a race which at first he appeared to have lost, Scobie could also remember winning a race which came close to being taken away from him; not in this instance by the stewards, but rather by the winning horse itself.

It was in a five furlong sprint at Hurst Park, where the straight ran into a cul-de-sac ended by a tall hedge, dividing the course from the back gardens of neighbouring houses. Scobie's mount, an easy winner, flashed past the post at great speed. Unfortunately not sharing the opinion that it was time to pull up and walk back to the winners' enclosure, continued to race on, quite impervious of his jockey's efforts to curb such over-enthusiasm, and on meeting the hedge, swiftly despatched his rider over to the other side.

Fortunately, apart from the uncomfortable experience of landing in a patch of brambles while dressed in thin riding silks, Scobie was unhurt. His more immediate problem, for there was no way to climb back over the hedge, was to reach the weighing room and weigh in before the allotted time elapsed and the race was awarded to another horse. He had no alternative but to go through the garden, past the house and along the main road leading to the entrance to the racecourse. As he made his way rather sheepishly towards the house, he could only hope that no irate figure would emerge, demanding to know just what a little man in fancy dress was doing in someone else's garden! Luck was with him, and he reached the road unobserved. Then, running back as fast as his paper thin riding boots would allow, he returned in time to save the situation; and to reflect on the fact that although his life as a professional jockey was rewarding, it was not without its share of aggravation! Yet in 1979, looking back to his days in the saddle, Scobie stated that only if a jockey goes on to become a trainer, does he begin to know the meaning of hard work.

Now, as Racing Manager to Ravi Tikkoo, his friends acknowledge the difficulty of his task. It is not always easy talking to trainers and co-ordinating where the horses are going to run. Trainers can find this hard to accept, but Scobie handles the situation well because he listens to what the other man has to say with attention and understanding.

This is the Scobie known to his friends. Adaptable, easy going and very much a man's man.

# SCOBIE AND THE LADIES

Were you to approach some of the "ladies" who figured in Scobie's life, you would find them unable to impart any information concerning his association with them. This apparent reticence would not be due to any modesty or discretion on their part, but rather to the fact that, as you may already have guessed, these particular "ladies" were the fillies whom he rode with such care and understanding during their racing days.

Two-year-old fillies are, of all mounts, the most notoriously difficult to ride, for they tend to be nervous and over-sensitive, although this is not invariably the case.

Perhaps one of the sweetest fillies Scobie ever rode was the lovely chestnut Festoon, who won The One Thousand Guineas in 1954; ridden by Scobie, she made all the running and won as she pleased. He counted her amongst the greatest of her sex.

Later there was Greengage, whom he rode to victory in all but one of her races. Yet before this he had a less happy encounter with another filly, Sayonara, who slipped and fell with him at Alexandra Park, only a few days after he had won The One Thousand Guineas on Festoon. This accident, the worst of his career, almost cost him his life.

He formed a happier association with Miss Arnhem, however, although she appears to have been a "lady" of strong likes and dislikes. Unfortunately for Eph Smith, who had ridden her to victory in a maiden race at Sandown, she developed a strong dislike of him, threw him if he mounted her, and even objected if he entered her box.

Scobie was asked to ride her in her next race, The Groombridge Handicap at Lingfield. Happily she accepted her new jockey at once, and together they won this race and several more the following year, when she won four races.

Scobie's ability to calm a fractious horse appeared sometimes to be almost magical. As on the occasion when the two-year-old Dolidu was taken to Kempton Park to run in The Rivermead Stakes and made a pathetic sight, standing in the parade ring, sweating and trembling as she waited to be mounted. Her trainer, Jackie Sirett, patted her neck and spoke gently to her, but these ministrations had little effect. Not that this was her first race, for she had already run into third place in The Rendlesham Stakes over the same course when ridden by Australian jockey Bill Williamson. This experience, however, had not given her a liking for either Kempton Park, or racing, and she appeared most distressed by the whole proceedings. Yet from the moment Scobie walked up to mount her, stroked her muzzle and slipped on to her back, she became a different animal, walked calmly around the ring and went out to make her way steadily to the start, even managing to run, yet again into third place. Certainly Scobie had a way with temperamental "ladies" of the Turf.

As for their human counterparts, there can be no denying that a number of these viewed Scobie with an interest that had little to do with his riding ability! If he was aware of this, he did not make it obvious, thereby adding to the mystique which was probably one of the main factors in his considerable appeal. Added to which he was a man at the height of his physical powers, approaching the zenith of his career, and if not handsome, his limitless charm more than compensated for that.

But there was to be no repetition of the romantic intrigues which had surrounded Steve Donoghue, for Scobie led a very different kind of domestic life to that great jockey of earlier days.

Donoghue and his friends were in the habit of visiting London night-clubs as much as three or four times a week, seeking the company of society beauties and chorus girls. He was the Peter Pan of Racing - the little boy who never grew up - he was feckless, warm-hearted and often irresponsible. On a voyage to South Africa in 1916, he met and fell in love with Lady Torrington. In any case his marriage had already broken down and an undefended divorce action was heard in London, at which Steve was granted a decree nisi, dissolving the marriage on the grounds of his wife Brigid's misconduct with a former jockey. Yet no scandal could lose him the affection of the Racing public who hero-worshipped him for his exploits as a jockey.

Scobie was a totally different character. Proud of his family man image, he would never become the subject of any scandal either on or off the Turf. But this could not prevent speculation among some of his admirers, who would have liked to have cast him in the role of lovable rogue, rather than solid citizen. Yet for all that their attitude was ambiguous, for had they felt quite certain that he measured up completely to either of these images, they would have been disappointed.

Scobie could lead a blameless life, yet his appearance and manner could suggest a flirtatiousness which was neither confirmed nor denied. The only way to keep everyone happy, was to keep them guessing. This Scobie did to perfection.

Sportsmen are frequently idolised by their public, even to the point of becoming cult figures. Yet outside of the Racing world, few would connect jockeys with this kind of hero-worship, for they are not waylaid by female fans, pulling off their ties or tugging out hair to keep as a souvenir. But even if the attention they command is more restrained than some other sportsmen have to contend with, this does not alter the fact that a few jockeys have reached "pop star" status. And however desirable such status may seem to those who have not achieved it, the demands and limitations imposed on one who has, would have many men wishing that they could retreat into comfortable obscurity; for one of the disadvantages of fame lies in the fact that every aspect of the personality is magnified and this applies to every fault as well as to every virtue.

If the man in the street makes a mistake, is careless or hurts someone's feelings, he will probably find himself involved in some minor conflict, usually of a temporary nature. Certainly he is unlikely to find his name in a newspaper as a result. Yet should a celebrity commit a comparable misdemeanour, should he put one foot out of place, he may very well find even the smallest indiscretion latched on to by the media and sometimes exaggerated out of all proportion. And a seemingly adoring public can be unexpectedly fickle.

It would be dishonest, even undesirable, to try to portray Scobie as a man without faults. Like everyone else he had his failings. Unlike them, as a man in the public eye, he could not hope that they would go unnoticed and he had to cope with the added disadvantage of being seen by many of the race-going public as a successor to Sir Gordon Richards; a formidable task indeed, for their temperaments were as different as their riding styles.

Sir Gordon, much loved by the public, had over the years acquired a reputation for being good-natured and benevolent; always ready to see the other man's point of view and ever the champion of good causes. A difficult image to follow.

Scobie, quite rightly, did not set out to live in the shadow of another man's image and any such comparisons must have been irksome to him. No one had more respect for Sir Gordon than Scobie, but they were, none the less, very different in character. Scobie had little patience with failure. It was almost as though he feared it might be contagious. His conviction that a person is responsible for their own fate led him away from any inclination to listen to hard luck stories, and he sometimes appeared lacking in compassion. Yet he could be the most compassionate of men if he felt the cause to be justified. But the decision had always to be his own; he could not be cajoled into acting against his will under any circumstances. If he was thought to be stubborn it was with reason, for he was obstinate to a fault. Yet it must be remembered that there are two sides to every coin, and without this trait in his character it is doubtful if we would have seen those great feats of determination which he displayed on the race track to the delight of his admirers.

If men came up against his obstinacy, and many did, it is in his dealings with women that this trait manifested itself most noticeably.

In order to analyse Scobie's attitude to women, it is essential to remember his origins. Born in Australia in the early part of this century and conditioned in early life to accepting attitudes very different from those existing in Britain or Europe at that time or later, it would have been strange indeed if he had not held different views from those prevalent in this country.

In the Australia of Scobie's youth, the sexes were segregated in a manner unknown in Britain. For example, a lady could not drink in a bar with men, not only because she thought it to be indelicate, but she was prohibited by law from doing so! In fact the attitudes to women were rigid in most aspects of everyday life and great stress was laid on the importance of ladies maintaining the highest moral standards.

From this environment Scobie was pitched into the British Racing world of the nineteen-fifties. A world largely populated by the British aristocracy who, at that time, saw nothing strange or immoral in marrying into "suitable" families in order to continue their dynasties and protect their entailed estates and, in many cases, keeping a mistress of their choice at the same time. This was seen as perfectly proper, even desirable behaviour. That society condoned these attitudes was largely due to the fact that at that period, marriage was considered to be indissoluble except in very exceptional circumstances.

Scobie was undisturbed, yet puzzled by these ideas. They were new to him amd existed in a strata of life well removed from his own. How any man could remain obligated towards a woman for any length of time, unless legally obliged to do so, was quite beyond his comprehension.

This attitude was not exclusive to Scobie. Rather it was the typical response of an antipodean male of that era and this would explain his unliberated attitude towards women. Unfortunately this was rarely apparent and he could sometimes convey the impression of a flirtatiousness for which there was no real foundation. Any lady unfortunate enough to misinterpret his intentions was quickly made aware of her mistake, for Scobie had no inhibitions about snubbing a woman who had displeased him and would not hesitate to humiliate her publicly if he saw fit to do so. This was particularly distressing when the lady treated in this cavalier fashion was innocent of any indiscretion. But Scobie often did not wait to find out if this were so, such was his dislike of the predatory female. He may have moved into a world where either sex felt at liberty to play the seducer, but this did not mean that he approved of the idea, yet with his "devil and saint" appearance, the attention he attracted was inevitable.

Once, while staying in Doncaster during the late seventies, Scobie faced an encounter which was to cause him some amusement and not a little heart searching.

Even Scobie, successful sportsman that he undoubtedly was, was sometimes given to moods in which optimism played no part. It was at just such a time that he found himself obliged to stay away from home for several days. Not that he disliked Doncaster, for he had a partiality for both the racecourse and the town itself. But he had just experienced a long losing run, a rare event for him, and his prospective mounts for the current meeting seemed unlikely to ʋring a badly needed change of luck.

Scobie suddenly felt every day of his fifty-odd years and, to add to his troubles, his wife, May, developed an attack of migraine severe enough to necessitate her immediate return to their Surrey home.

If he felt sorry for himself, his state of mind apparently detracted in no way from his powers of attraction. For at teatime that same afternoon, an attractive Racing lady, less than half his age, made no secret of the fact that she found his company and conversation most agreeable.

Perhaps he needed a boost to his morale or he was unmindful of the implications when, on discovering that the girl would be dining in the very hotel where he was staying, he invited her to join him for a drink in his room after dinner.

It may be that he had really meant to say, before dinner. But the invitation was accepted so readily and with such obvious pleasure as to make it virtually impossible to withdraw.

Almost at once Scobie began to regret his indiscretion and the dinner taken in the company of close friends that evening lost much of its anticipated pleasure as he tried to think of a way out of his self-inflicted dilemma, while at the same time trying to play the attentive host and conceal from the assembled company the fact that all was not well.

By the end of the second course he had still no idea of how he could extricate himself from what he now felt sure would be a most embarrassing situation.

The answer, when it came, was almost literally handed to him on a plate. The waitress serving at his table that evening had, throughout his stay in the hotel, treated Scobie with an almost outrageous flirtatiousness which both knew was not meant to be taken seriously and which each enjoyed for that very reason. This lady, a buxom, kindly, North-country woman, seemed at that moment to be the answer to Scobie's prayers.

Excusing himself to his guests, he slipped away from the table and soon found the lady he was looking for. Feeling somewhat sheepish, he explained that he was expecting a young lady to visit him after dinner and was a little uneasy about her coming in his room as he was afraid that she might stay longer than he had intended and his association might be misunderstood. Would it, he asked, be possible for the waitress to come to his room some ten minutes or so after the arrival of his visitor?

Fortunately for Scobie, he was already something of a hero to his chosen conspirator and she happily agreed to assist him by arriving at the appointed time on the pretext of bringing or removing something from his room.

The second half of the meal was a more relaxed affair than the first and at the end Scobie did not linger longer than was absolutely necessary.

He had been back in his room for about five minutes when he heard the anticipated knock at his door, which he opened to find his visitor, well dressed, smiling and totally unaware of how very unwelcome she was at that moment. Scobie showed her to a chair, poured wine into two glasses and seated himself opposite to his guest at what he hoped was a reasonable, formal distance. After a few moments of polite conversation, Scobie began to feel uneasy. What, he wondered, could he do if his ally failed to arrive? Surely ten minutes must have elapsed since the arrival of his smiling, disturbing visitor?

At this point the situation began to look like turning into a bedroom farce, for the girl asked if she might use the bathroom and no sooner had she disappeared from view, than Scobie heard the knock he had been hoping for at the outer door. On opening he found the waitress facing him; "She's gone into the bathroom" he hissed, reducing his voice to a whisper. Then, very loudly, hoping to be heard through the bathroom door, he almost shouted "Can you come back in a few minutes?" whereupon his would-be rescuer whispered something in the affirmative.

A moment later, his by now very unwelcome visitor re-entered the room. She was no longer smiling, in fact she now wore a rather guarded expression and asked "Was that a woman at the door?" Scobie said "Yes, the chambermaid and she's coming back soon." He then suggested that it might be better if they parted before her return as it might not look nice for a lady to be in his room at such a late hour. As it was not a very late hour, this appeared to arouse some suspicions, and unfortunately led to his young guest accusing him of making what she implied were unsavoury assignations with servants, before leaving with an air of one who has been deeply offended.

Scobie sank into a chair, relief flooding over him. But not for long. What, he wondered, would happen if the waitress had by some chance misunderstood his request to her to visit his room? In the end, he had decided that if the worst came to be, he would, rather than be pursued like some latter day Casanova, go and sleep on the floor of his chauffeur's room. When the tap on his door finally came, he was ready. Opening it no wider than necessary, he put his head out and quickly said "It's all right, she's gone." Then he shut the door and thankfully settled down to a solitary, but peaceful night thinking, as he drifted into sleep, that his conspirator, who had looked undeniably taken aback when he so quickly closed the door, would no doubt be placated by the handsome tip which he intended to bestow on her before he left to return home.

That he was perfectly entitled to his own views on this subject is undeniable. It is, however, regrettable that he did not handle such situations with more finesse and a little more thought for the feelings of any lady who incited his displeasure. Yet he would not have considered that an injustice had been done. His inability to regard women as sexually equal would have prevented any such consideration.

This is not to say that Scobie disliked women. On the contrary he was as susceptible to their charms as any other man, but he had a tidy mind, he liked to have a place for everything and everything in its place. Ladies were not exempt from this rule, and in his eyes, a real lady was one who kept her charms to herself, unless asked to do otherwise. Nor did the female sex escape his strictures in the professional field. After he retired from the saddle to become a racehorse trainer, faced with two applicants, one female and one male, when a vacancy for a stable lad arose; the girl might be a talented horsewoman and the man no more than a mediocre rider, yet almost invariably the male applicant would get the job.

Perhaps, and it does seem very probable, the answer lies in his own susceptibility coupled with the influence of his early environment. Yet such was his love of a celebration, that sometimes his sexual prejudices were set aside, as on the occasion when Miss Norah Wilmot became the first woman to officially train a winner under Jockey Club rules. This happened at Brighton on 3rd August 1966, when Miss P.K. Wolf's "Pat" came home a winner, and the dull rainy afternoon was brightened by the smiling faces in the unsaddling enclosure where Scobie was one of the first to shake the hand of a delighted Miss Wilmot and offer his congratulations, showing, as he sometimes did, that in moments of triumph, either his or theirs, he could be magnanimous to both men and women when the occasion merited his acclaim.

His attitude to women could be puzzling yet, when in their company, he was almost invariably charming and courteous.

However, this did not always ensure an unqualified success and one lady owner, took some pleasure in deflating his ego after he had the misfortune to fall from one of her horses in a race at Newbury.

Scobie, who had been taken to a nearby hospital for X-ray examinations, was found to have sustained only minor injuries and was allowed to go home the following morning.

A few days later the owner telephoned to enquire as to the state of Scobie's health. May answered the 'phone and asked if the caller would like to speak to Scobie personally. Soon he was on the line and, on learning that the lady he was speaking to was the owner of the horse from which he had recently fallen, he said, rather sarcastically, "Thank you for your letters of condolence and for the fruit and flowers," to which he instantly received the reply "I don't send fruit or flowers to jockeys for falling off my horses!"

The same owner was heard to say on another occasion "The British sent their misfits and criminals out to Australia a hundred years ago and today their descendents return to us as Flat race jockeys." Which might make one wonder why she should employ any of them to ride her horses. She answered this question herself when saying "Scobie Breasley was a great rider, probably the best we have ever seen or, perhaps, will ever see." Then she added ominously "When he was trying!"

As with his races, so it was with the ladies; he could not win them all. Nor, as far as the ladies were concerned, did he wish to.

His "family man" image was never called into question. A devoted husband, father and grandfather, Scobie had no need to stress this point with anyone who knew him. He put a high value on a happy home and family life. That this side of his life was as much a success story as his professional accomplishments cannot be doubted. If further confirmation were needed, one only need turn to his wife, May, who said after many years of marriage "He is an easy man to live with and a wonderful father. In fact, Scobie is the best choice I ever made." Who could ask for more?

# PRELUDE TO DEPARTURE

They called him ageless, this jockey who had come to England with the intention of retiring after a year of riding in this country and who, seventeen years later, in 1967, was riding as brilliantly as at any time in his career.

By now Scobie was fifty-three years old and he and Sir Gordon were still going on happily at Whitsbury; if either was beginning to feel his age there was no sign of this. In fact 1967 saw them achieve many successes together, not the least of these being with Reform, who started by getting narrowly beaten by Play High in The Greenham Stakes at Newbury, but soon opened his winning account in The St. James Stakes at Epsom on Derby Day, thus relieving some of the disappointment felt by Scobie and his Guv'nor when Dart Board was beaten into third place by Royal Palace and Ribocco in the colts classic. Reform might well have been a Derby winner himself; he was certainly one of the best horses ever trained by Sir Gordon Richards; it is a pity that he appeared to lack promise in his early days and as a result was never entered for either The Two Thousand Guineas or The Derby. One of the reasons Reform was so sadly misjudged in his early days was due to his slightly malformed forelegs and unprepossessing appearance as a foal. Yet he went on to win no less than six races as a two-year-old and at three, after his Epsom victory, he was soon in the winner's enclosure again when beating 20-1 outsider Chinwag by a head in The St. James's Palace Stakes at Ascot. Scobie came in for some severe criticism for his riding of this race, as thinking he had victory firmly in his grasp, he eased Reform inside the final furlong, not having noticed the great run being put in by Chinwag, who almost caught him on the line. It was said that a collec-

111

tive sigh of relief could be heard all over the course when the result of the photograph showed Reform to be the winner. His trainer observed "Scobie would have been on the first boat to Melbourne if it had gone the other way!" Sir Gordon told Scobie that he had nearly given him a heart attack, to which his jockey replied "I very nearly gave myself one!" Nothing was left to chance in The Sussex Stakes at Goodwood on 26th July when Reform came home a comfortable winner. But in The Wills Mile at the same course a month later he was beaten by a length by St. Chad to whom he was conceding five pounds. Scobie was inclined to blame the moderate pace for this defeat. Be that as it may, on 30th September at Ascot Reform put up a great performance when winning The Queen Elizabeth II Stakes by ten lengths from Track Spare, but his greatest triumph came in The Champion Stakes at Newmarket on 21st October when he beat Taj Dewan by two lengths, with the Derby winner, Royal Palace, third and Pia fourth. In winning this race looking so fit and well at a time when many horses were starting to look very wintry, Reform paid a striking tribute to his trainer's skill. His owner, Michael Sobell, who also owned Dart Board, was delighted with him.

Reform retired to stud at the end of 1967 - a season in which he was never out of the frame - and since then has sired many winners, including an Oaks winner, Polygamy, and Admetus who won The Washington International.

It had been a good year. Scobie notched up a total of one hundred and nine winners. Already he was looking to the year ahead with pleasant anticipation, for Lady Beaverbrook, widow of the famous newspaper proprietor, had asked Sir Gordon, who had finished second to Noel Murless in the trainers' table that year, to train some of her horses in the coming season and Scobie expected to bring the brown and maple green colours to the winner's enclosure many times in the days ahead. In the expectation he was not to be disappointed.

Scobie returned rather late to the Flat Racing scene in 1968, not putting in an appearance until April 5th at Ascot. He had missed the opening meeting at Doncaster, where his old rival Doug Smith, the man who had relegated him to second place in the jockeys' championships of 1958 and 1959, had saddled his first runner as a trainer and had the pleasure of seeing this colt, Owen Anthony, come home the winner of The First Apprentice Handicap, making a happy start to the season for this popular ex-jockey.

For Scobie, the early part of this season appears to have been considerably less propitious, for on May 24th at the Bath meeting, Miss Rosewyn threw him while going down to the start and not content with this unladylike behaviour, she then kicked him in the head.

If we look back over Scobie's record of accidents over the years, and he does appear to have suffered an inordinate number of these for a Flat race jockey, we will find that most occurred in the early part of the season and some of the worst took place in the month of May, including the terrible accident involving Sayonara at Alexandra Park in 1954 which came close to ending the Breasley story for ever. Happily the incident at Bath in 1968 was not so serious; Scobie was soon back in the saddle. He had no classic engagements that year, with the exception of Ileana who was unplaced in The One Thousand Guineas.

The Derby this year was won by Lester Piggott riding Sir Ivor. Piggott went on to ride a classic double when later in the season he won The St. Leger on Ribero. Both these colts were engaged in The Irish Sweeps Derby. Piggott elected to ride Ribero, a brother of Ribocco who had won the race the previous year and although Ribero had been badly beaten by Connaught at Ascot, he won

The Irish Sweeps Derby by two lengths from Sir Ivor ridden by Liam Ward, with Val d'Aoste third. It was felt that Sir Ivor had run well below his true form and his trainer, Vincent O'Brien, made the bold decision to run him in The Eclipse Stakes at Sandown the following Saturday.

There were five runners for The Eclipse including the formidable Royal Palace, winner of the 1967 Derby and Two Thousand Guineas, who already this year had won The Coronation Cup; Taj Dewan second to Royal Palace in The Guineas finished in front of him in The Champion Stakes and won The Prix Ganay at four.

Rounding the final bend Saint-Martin took Taj Dewan to the front, still a long way from home, yet inside the final furlong Taj Dewan showed no sign of weakening, while Sir Ivor was under pressure and failing to accelerate. It looked as if Royal Palace had a bit too much to do; nevertheless, he was battling on to cheers of encouragement from the crowd. It was a photograph between Royal Palace and Taj Dewan with almost everyone convinced that Taj Dewan had won. However, the camera showed that Royal Palace had scored by a very narrow margin. It was said to be the most exciting Eclipse since 1903 when Ard Patrick beat Sceptre with the Triple Crown winner, Rock Sand, third. Those three great horses won eight classic races between them.

Lester Piggott blamed the going which was very hard for Sir Ivor's defeat. With only a week to go before he was due to run in The Prix de l'Arc de Triomphe, he was entered for the Prix Henry Delamarre at Longchamp, but failed by half a length to beat Prince Sao. In The Arc Sir Ivor ran a fine race although he was beaten three lengths by Vaguely Noble. Thirteen days later he lined up for The Champion Stakes at Newmarket, run over his best distance of a mile and a quarter, where he won easily from Locris. He then tra-

velled to America and beat Czar Alexander and
Fort Marcy in The Washington International at
Laurel. Sir Ivor then retired to stud. He was
voted the 1968 Horse of the Year, much to the
chagrin of the admirers of Royal Palace who was
unbeaten at four and had fairly defeated Sir Ivor
the only time they met.

On the whole the year was going along rather
quietly for Scobie. In fact it was not the most exhilarating year for British Racing in general. There
were no great excitements at Goodwood and it was
felt that English owners were being lured away from
the Sussex course by the high level of prize money
at Deauville. For instance, in 1968 The Goodwood
Cup won by Ovaltine was worth three thousand, two
hundred and fifty-nine pounds to the winning owner,
while Pardallo earned fourteen thousand, four
hundred and thirty-nine pounds when winning The
Prix Kergorlay, and the Prix Morny was worth nineteen thousand, six hundred and thirty-two pounds to
Princeline, with The Richmond Stakes won by Tudor
Music worth six thousand, four hundred and twenty-
one pounds. Goodwood retained much of its popu-
larity with the Racing public, though the social side
suffered due to staffing difficulties in the large
houses in the surrounding countryside.

It was at Goodwood that the shock came -
Scobie announced his decision to retire. It should
not have been a shock, after all Scobie was fifty-
four and had threatened to retire almost twenty
years earlier. Yet nonetheless it shook the Racing
world, for it had been so long since he had spoken
of giving up riding and no one ever spoke of retirement to him, almost as if they were afraid of
putting any such idea into his head, although two
years previously his wife, May, was quoted in the
Press as saying "I wish Scobie would retire, but he
would miss it all so much. It would not be a fair
thing to ask of him."

It was very difficult for May Breasley to prevent herself from trying to persuade Scobie that he should give up his career as a jockey. She knew that her opinions and feelings carried a lot of weight with her husband and it says much for her self control and desire to put his feelings before her own that much of the time she kept her thoughts concerning his retirement to herself. Often it was an ordeal; she could not bear to watch the finish of a race in which he was riding. There had been too many accidents and she had lost confidence in his powers. That she was not from a Racing background herself only added to the difficulties. The other Racing wives were unlikely to be understanding, mostly raised among horses; her own fear of these animals would be incomprehensible to them. In 1970, recalling her wedding day she said "I knew nothing about horses then and even now my knowledge is scant."

The announcement of Scobie's impending retirement may have saddened the Racing world, but for his wife it was as though a great weight, carried for so long, was suddenly lifted. At last the fear of yet another accident would be gone for ever.

It would not, however, mean the end of contact with horses, for Scobie had decided to take out a trainer's licence. In earlier days May had said that she expected Scobie would suddenly decide to retire from the saddle and devote his considerable energies to his beloved game of golf. Perhaps this was wishful thinking, for on reflection, his wife, along with everyone close to him, knew that horses were an integral part of this man. He could not let them go; for they would not let him go.

Once the momentous decision had been reached, it seemed as though the days flew by all too quickly for Scobie's admirers. It was almost as if the weight lifted from his wife's shoulders had been added to their own, for they did not live in fear of his accidents, were rather surprised when he suffered them, and still believed in his abilities.

116

Now every winner counted as a vintage performance as the feeling that they would not see his like again grew stronger with every passing day.

The last meeting of the 1968 Flat Racing season was scheduled to take place at Haydock Park. If Scobie had to go, and by now even his staunchest supporters had accepted the inevitable, their dearest wish was to see him go out on a winner.

Since his arrival in Britain Scobie had seen many changes take place in Racing; and not always for the better. When starting stalls were first introduced he viewed them with some misgivings. This was understandable for Scobie was a past master in the art of jumping a sprinter off smartly at the start. However, once he accustomed himself to this innovation, he thought it fairer than the old method of starting tapes.

Other changes were less desirable and many famous colours began to disappear from the British Turf. Racing had been called The Sport of Kings and sometimes still is. But it was for many years the aristocracy who dominated the sport. Racing interests had been handed on from father to son, but during Scobie's years in England this pattern began to change. Crushing death duties resulted in many a famous Racing family fading from the sport as horses were dispersed on the death of their owners. New trends were developing, the titled owner was on the way out and the tycoons of industry were on the way in. Racing was in danger of becoming big business which had nothing to do with sport. Many said this had already happened.

To be fair to the new crop of owners, many could not afford to regard Racing simply as a sport. The horses had to earn their keep.

Owners have always been a mixed bunch at the best of times. Scobie had ridden for many types of owner, but the owner of the horse he intended to be his last mount in public was a man whose integrity, knowledge and love of the sport could not be faulted; the Racing journalist and commentator Mr. Peter O'Sullevan.

The Vernons Sprint Cup was to be run on the last day of the 1968 Flat Race season. The winner of this race over the past two seasons was that great sprinter Be Friendly. In fact Scobie had ridden him to victory in that race the previous year and both owner and jockey felt it would make a most fitting end to forty years of brilliant race riding.

Peter O'Sullevan had loved horses from his earliest days. Born in County Kerry, that part of Ireland noted for its fine horses, the young O'Sullevan grew up in a horse-orientated society. His father, Colonel John Joseph O'Sullevan, was a well known steward and popular figure in the Irish Racing world so it is not really surprising that even at the age of eight the boy had decided to aim for a career as a Racing journalist. Many boys of this age will name their future career with very strong conviction, but will have changed their minds many times before reaching the age when a definite choice must be made. Not so with Peter O'Sullevan; he knew from the beginning what he wanted to do and the Racing world can count itself fortunate that he held fast to that early decision.

Although athletic, having ridden since early childhood and later proving himself a force to be reckoned with on the football field, he nonetheless did not enjoy the best of health, having been troubled with asthma ever since birth. This unfortunate affliction was responsible for his leaving Charterhouse and being sent to the College Alpin in Switzerland. There he developed the flawless French accent that would stand him in good stead in years to come when a big field at Longchamp or Chantilly would present no problem for him. Having been turned down by the fighting services, O'Sullevan spent a busier and often more dangerous time than many a man who had been accepted. Working with the Rescue Service in Chelsea during the worst period of the Blitz, he soon acquired a reputation for bravery. Going into blazing buildings to rescue injured people, he seemed not to care if a bomb exploded under his feet or a building caved in on top of him. Modestly he claims that these dare-devil tactics were due more to a temporary indifference to life than to courage on his part.

As a young man, the asthma from which he had always suffered developed into acne which was severe enough to necessitate a year's stay in hospital; at the end of this time he was told that nothing more could be done for his condition. There followed an indescribably painful period of avoiding brightly lit places and direct communication with fellow human beings. It was not a happy time and in his need for some form of communication he turned to painting and literature, thereby laying the foundation for the interests that would sustain and restore him in the busy life that lay ahead, the happier days, when most of his time would be taken up with one sort of communication or another as he pleased his audiences with both the written and the spoken word.

That he put those dark days to good use will come as no surprise to anyone who has met him, for Peter instantly comes across as a man who would always turn adversity into advantage if it is humanly possible to do so.

As an owner he is patient and enthusiastic, ever conscious that owners must be eternal optimists. He should know, for he had to wait fifteen years for his first winner, Pretty Fair at Windsor on March 11th 1954. In these days when Racing is often more a business than a sport, it is refreshing to find an owner like Peter O'Sullevan.

Be Friendly was to give his owner the happiest Racing experience of his life when he won the 1966 Vernons Sprint Cup. But his story begins before

119

that auspicious November day.   Peter's charming
grey filly Friendly Again had proved herself to be
so genuine that when her yearling half-brother was
sent to the Newmarket Sales, both Peter and his
partner, Stephen Raphael, were keen to buy the
chestnut colt and got him for two thousand, eight
hundred guineas.   He was by Skymaster out of
Friendly Again's dam, Lady Sliptic.   They called
him Be Friendly.

It was not long before trainer, Cyril Mitchell,
realized that this colt was something out of the
ordinary.  In March he worked Be Friendly with his
good five-year-old Espeekay.  The two-year-old was
giving the older horse fifteen pounds meeting him
on forty-six pounds worse than weight for age.  He
ran Espeekay into the ground.  A few days later at
Lingfield, Espeekay won the six-furlong Canterbury
Handicap from seventeen rivals at odds of 20-1.

Be Friendly made his debut in The Apple-
blossom Stakes at Lingfield on May 14th 1966.  He
had suffered from sore shins and though still backward was able to run into third place at 25-1.
Jimmy Lindley who rode the colt on his first outing
in public, thought well of him and told his owners
not to worry, he was sure this young horse would
go on to greater things.

In July Scobie rode Be Friendly for the first
time, bringing him home the winner of The Wren
Stakes at Kempton and later that month on July
30th they won The Box Hill Stakes at Epsom.  The
colt was then ridden by apprentice Colin Williams
in The Highclere Nursery at Newbury in September
where he was beaten into second place by Early
Turn, but this capable boy rode him to victory a
month later in The Wantage Nursery Stakes over
the same course.

It had been a busy season for this two-year-old
but his biggest test that year was yet to come.  Be
Friendly was entered for the Vernons Sprint at
Haydock.  It was an innovation to have two-year-

olds in this race and this year the opposition was formidable. The four-year-old Lucasland had won The Diadem Stakes and The July Cup; Dondeen had been runner-up in both those contests; Green Park had won Ascot's Cornwallis Stakes and Potier, Kamundu and Go Shell were winners respectively the previous year of The Steward's Cup, Ayr Gold Cup and The Portland Handicap. Could an apprentice-ridden two-year-old take on such an impressive line up and hope to win? Popular opinion at the time thought it unlikely. Even Jimmy Lindley, who thought well of the gallant Be Friendly, told Peter O'Sullevan "I'm afraid your chap has no earthly chance whatever of beating Green Park."

On Friday afternoon Peter visited Be Friendly in the racecourse stables. He found him to be in sparkling form and thought once again what a smashing young horse this chestnut with a white blaze and one white sock was. Back at his hotel he filed copy to the Daily Express napping his colt to win.

After a sleepless night, the owner and the jockey were out walking the course by seven a.m. Discussing riding tactics, they decided that in the soft going it would be an advantage to come over to the stand side, but having measured with a string, they knew that such a move would cost one and a half lengths. Even so, Colin Williams was in favour of pursuing this seemingly extravagant course.

Peter had the added anxiety of having to commentate on the race. That afternoon in his box high above the racecourse his throat felt so dry that he wondered if any sound would come out at all. Then they were off, and anyone listening to the B.B.C. coverage, hearing that so familiar voice commentating with accuracy and complete impartiality, would never have guessed that they were hearing the voice of a man about to realise the dream of a lifetime. When the horses reached the

121

turn, Colin started to tack over to the stand side. Russ Maddock on Green Park shouted: "Get in, boy." Colin shouted back "I'm going over." There was a bit of barging, but Be Friendly made it and passed the post two lengths ahead of Green Park.

All eyes were on the commentary box; smiling faces turned upwards to the winning owner who, still in headphones, was telling millions of viewers: "First No.13, Be Friendly, owned by Mr. P.J. O'Sullevan; trained by Cyril Mitchell and ridden by apprentice Colin Williams." Then after naming the minor placings, he quietly excused himself and went down to lead in the winner.

The following year Be Friendly won the same race, this time with Scobie in the saddle. There could not have been a more exhilarating end to the season for the brilliant three-year-old and his connections. In March he had won the Two Thousand Guineas Trial Stakes at Kempton and went on to win the prestigious King's Stand Stakes at Royal Ascot. He was partnered by Scobie in both these races. Then came the long journey to Scotland and victory in The Ayr Gold Cup, when ridden by Geoff Lewis.

Now it was 1968 and Scobie, hoping to make his last ride a winner, knew that in Be Friendly he had a horse who could make that dream a reality. Earlier that season they had come second to Manacle in a race at Kempton, with that good colt Porto Bello behind them in third place. In July, Be Friendly, ridden again by Geoff Lewis, had dead-heated with Klaizia in The Prix du Gros-Chene at Chantilly and the same partnership won The Prix de L'Abbaye de Longchamp on 6th October.

What a triumph it would be if Be Friendly could win The Vernons Sprint Cup for the third year running, making a hat trick for him and a double for Scobie.

All the colt's preparation on the home gallops was now centred upon achieving this end. Excitement mounted with every passing day.   Cyril Mitchell intended to have his charge tuned to perfect pitch in time for the big day at Haydock. And Be Friendly was responding all the time, almost as if he knew what was expected of him.

The morning of the penultimate day of the 1968 Flat Racing season dawned cold and bleak at Haydock Park.   No course catches the end of season atmosphere quite like this Lancastrian track with its leafless trees standing stark against the skyline.   This year it was more poignant than usual, for shortly the drab Winter paddock would be splashed with the bright colours of jockeys' silks and Scobie would be amongst them for the last time.   The board with the name A. BREASLEY painted in white letters on a black background would be removed from its slot in the jockeys' number board for ever; taken down to stand like one of those leafless paddock trees, though unlike them, it would not regain its former glory in the coming Spring.

But still there was Friday racing to go through before The Vernons Sprint, the main race on Saturday's card.   Scobie's last ride on that Friday was the filly Arrandora Star, who he was riding for Jack Clayton.   She ran a fair race, but got beaten by Lester on Notonia.

Scobie was late leaving the course.   For weeks his autograph and photos had been much in demand. Mostly it was the Press:   "Would you stand over here Mr. Breasley"; "Can we have a smile please?" and good naturedly Scobie obliged.   At this last meeting there were more demands than ever.   A nearby policeman observed "Pity they are not all as nice as him."   Then an admirer presented Scobie with an album of photographs showing not only his great mounts and classic victories, but snaps taken at random of horses of every calibre ridden by him.

Back at The Greyhound, the hotel near the course where he was staying, Scobie was in a reflective mood. It was difficult to believe that his forty years as a jockey were almost over. A 'phone call from a friend reminded him that tomorrow would not be without an element of sadness. But he put the thought from him, for a new career as a trainer lay ahead, the days would be full and the horses never far away. It was time for a change and with this thought in mind, he bathed, put on a well cut suit and went down to join Peter O'Sullevan at dinner.

Of course the conversation centred on The Vernons Sprint. Be Friendly was reported to be in great shape and ready to run the race of his life. Neither of these two great men of the Turf had the slightest doubt that the next day would be a day to celebrate. A day that would see the famous black and yellow colours first past the post yet again.

Peter and Scobie, so very different in character, had grown close through their mutual love of horses. Now like two happy conspirators, they relished the prospect of the coming race as they enjoyed an excellent meal, washed down with a good wine, before retiring in the rather vain hope of getting a good night's sleep.

Scobie woke early, he often did and consequently he had seen many a misty November morning. Yet looking back, that morning in Lancashire did not seem unduly misty, with nothing more than a light haze hanging over the countryside. After breakfast it was much the same; Scobie read the newspapers and prepared for the day ahead which seemed so like all the other days when he had followed the same routine before a day's racing. It all seemed so familiar, yet this day would be like no other that had gone before it, because he would be riding in public for the last time. He did not dwell on the sadness of the occasion, but rather turned his thoughts to the prospect of ending his riding career on a winner, as his confidence in Be Friendly led him to believe that this was as near to a racing certainty as he could hope for.

Then the time came to leave for the course. It was no very great distance, yet with every yard the mist was thickening and on reaching the course the visibility had deteriorated so much that it would have to lift quickly if racing were to take place.

They had to believe that the visibility would improve. Neither owner, trainer, nor jockey could bring themselves to think otherwise. Mid-way through the afternoon there had still been no racing, yet even then the stewards had not officially abandoned the meeting. The jockeys were already weighed out for The Vernons Sprint when at last all hope of a miracle was given up and the announcement came that the meeting had been abandoned. The form book for 1968 tells the reader "Meeting abandoned due to fog". How cold those statistics seem to anyone who knows of the hopes built around that November day, but "Dream abandoned due to fog" would never appear in any form book.

So when Scobie rode Arrandora Star into second place behind Notonia, he was, although he did not know it, riding in public for the last time. Instead of going out in a blaze of glory on a brilliant sprinter, he finished his riding career coming in second on a moderate filly. Yet while a cruel fate robbed Scobie and all Be Friendly connections of the prize on which their hearts had been set, some of the jockey's admirers, while sympathizing with all concerned, could not help feeling rather relieved at having been spared that dreaded moment when Scobie would have mounted Be Friendly and ridden out of the parade ring and down to the start for the last time.

The following season Scobie took over the South Hatch stable at Epsom. After a few years of training there, he became private trainer to oil tanker tycoon, Ravi Tikkoo. When Tikkoo took his horses out of England in order to be based in France, Scobie accompanied him and for some time trained at Chantilly. But soon the Tikkoo string was on the move again, this time to America and once again Scobie pulled up his roots and went to where he was needed. He was to return to South Hatch and British Racing in 1979. Both Scobie and his wife May were happy to be back in the country they had come to think of as home.

It is as a jockey that Scobie Breasley will be best remembered. He was already a mature and experienced rider when he left Australia in 1950; but his greatest achievements were realized on the British Turf.

Back in 1875, The Wagga Wagga Advertiser printed the following:

> "Centrally placed as is Wagga Wagga, in a splendid district (possessing within itself all the germs of a great prosperity) her destinies guided by men of intelligence, speculative enterprise and indomitable perseverance, her advancement in the future is (humanly speaking) assured and certain. In addition to those merely local, yet stimulating and powerful advantages, her geographical position is in every sense so commanding and apparent, that the prophetic spirits of the times foretell a great social and commercial future. With men some are born great, some achieve greatness and some have greatness thrust upon them; and so it is with Wagga, so placed, so surrounded by circumstances which must propel her forward on the high road of success, that she must become great in the ordinary course of natural events - we say to her - "God speed! Ride on and prosper."

A proud and optimistic tribute to the town of

Wagga Wagga, but much of it could easily have been a prophetic reference to one of her most illustrious sons as yet unborn - Arthur Edward (Scobie) Breasley - who would first see the light of day some thirty years after this was printed. They said "Ride on and prosper" - he did just that.

Scobie never sought the limelight. Inevitably he attracted much attention on account of his ability and his undeniable charisma. The search to find what lay behind the public image leads us, in Scobie's case, to the conclusion that here was a man with whom we could easily identify, a very human person, not always infallible and really much like you or me - yet set apart from us by his genius. Probably one of the greatest riders the world has ever seen or ever will see. Scobie has not ridden as a jockey for more than a decade, yet even now, those who delighted in his artistry find it almost inconceivable that we will not see him ride again - except on the many occasions when he rides in our memories and through our dreams.

******